Author's Background

As a "habitual criminal" and recovering addict, Ned Rollo takes the issue of success after prison very personally. As a nationally respected teacher and counselor, he is equally concerned that others survive and prosper beyond the madness of the criminal justice system.

The author has been active on both sides of the law for 36 years. First, as a former prisoner with four felony convictions including manslaughter, possession of narcotics, and two counts of federal firearms violations. He served over five years in federal and state prisons from 1966 to 69 and 1974 to 77 and required many more years to rebuild his life from scratch after release.

Second, Rollo is a 1971 graduate of Roosevelt University in Chicago and has spent over 23 years teaching self-help skills to offenders and their families. In 1979 he founded OPEN, INC., a non-profit agency in Dallas, Texas, to provide training and support to people caught up in the punishment industry. Today his work is in use across the nation, offering a beacon of hope and direction to millions of men and women who carry the label of "criminal" with them to the grave.

This book is built on the author's direct experience combined with the shared insight of over 35,000 offenders and loved ones he has worked with. In addition, he has learned a great deal from the many corrections professionals he has met and trained. As a result, Ned Rollo knows *exactly* what a person released from a cage has to do to build a life of quality and self-respect. He doesn't lay down any fairy tales about how easy life will be after prison. Instead, he tells the truth: reality on reality's terms. In the process, he gives a sometimes painful but always encouraging view of what it takes to construct a productive, rewarding future.

Rollo makes it clear that the real challenge of release is not just to survive but to prepare for future achievement and satisfaction. Along with advice on avoiding the traps an ex-con faces, he offers a fresh, clean way to re-define yourself as a person worthy of respect. *The result is a valuable path to dignity and pride!*

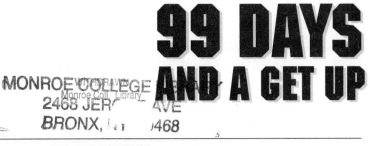

99 DAYS AND A GET UP

Guide to Success Following Release for Inmates and Their Loved Ones

3rd Edition

Ned Rollo

Executive Director
OPEN, INC.

OPEN, INC. Information Series
Series Editor
Katherine S. Greene

OPEN INC.

It is possible to travel slowly but surely into the depths of consciousness and there transform our personality. We can actually make a new person of ourselves; we can become the kind of person we dream of being. When we have the daring and determination to make such changes, a tremendous beneficial power is released into our lives. Slowly and gradually, but without fail, that power will transform our world.

Eknath Easwaran

Contents

CONTENTS

Introduction

Preparing for the Streets

"They lined us up buck naked in a cold, driving rain just inside the Sally Port gate...then ol' Captain Blue Eyes comes out in a yellow slicker and begins to shout: 'In case you are too stupid to know it, this here is Hell – and it's my job to see just how much heat you bastards can take!!'"

Obviously you don't have a lot of warm, fuzzy feelings about the day you fell off into the joint. It is a day to be remembered, however, because it was the beginning of a hard, painful journey. And no matter how much time you end up doing, it will affect the rest of your life in countless ways.

After your body was rudely dumped at the sally port in shackles, it took 18 to 24 months for your mind to really join it. Even then, it came kicking and screaming because it had to, just to survive. So your head came off the streets a little at a time, slowly shifting focus from free world issues to the sick trash that makes a cell block tick. And gradually, through hard knocks, you learned what's up and how to cope in a human zoo.

A lot of changes have come and gone since then, one heartbeat at a time. Sometimes you weren't sure your heart could take it ... like when the divorce papers arrived, your appeal was denied, or the news came of your father's death. Every inmate has had to face such moments, when your whole being seems to explode and you find yourself adrift in space, cut off from the universe. In those moments of silent screams, you feel yourself changing in ways that no words can ever express.

And here you are today – maybe two years later, maybe twenty – still looking through bars and wanting OUT. But now relief is finally around the corner. Sometime over the next year the Man is going to cut you loose. As you prepare for life after prison, you need to understand that it will hold both challenges and opportunities. Just as you went through extreme hardships when you drove up, you will have to face *equally* powerful changes after they kick you out.

Why? Three basic reasons: first, life in the world is demanding from jump street, even if you've never been locked up. Second, the world has changed, and you were not there to change with it. Last, *you* have changed in ways that don't fit into life in the community. Therefore, many of your thoughts, feelings, and concerns will need to be adjusted to the world you are re-entering.

So take a deep breath and face the truth: it takes an ex-con at least two years after release to get his or her feet on solid ground and mind focused on the realities of life in the free world. *You* may need even more time to adjust, depending on how long you've been down and how much pain and poison you have absorbed. The longer you've been away, the more you have to re-learn and the longer it will take to reach a point of confidence and comfort. This is not good or bad, it's simply how it works; you need to understand and prepare for it.

An ex-con has a lot to learn on many levels, and learning requires time and effort. As with all major changes in life, this one demands a special price, dues that have to be paid. If you walk out believing you can get your head and heart right overnight, just by sheer will power and wishful thinking, *you are setting yourself up to fail!* Success takes *time,* it takes *work,* and it takes *patience –* so get ready to pay the price!

Why Bother?

"There is infinitely more to life than being a pet poodle with a number. You can grow far past this harsh, nasty game."

The first few years after release are so demanding that a person has to maintain a strong, constant motivation to "go on no matter what." Yet this is easier said than done. You will get kicked in the teeth time after time – and each time you have to

force yourself to get up and go on.

This is especially hard if all you can see ahead is more of the same day-to-day survival. So how do you keep yourself going? What's the point, when everything is boring or bleak? Isn't there more to life than just surviving and staying out of the joint? Take my word for it, the price you pay following release is worth it. Beyond this period of mere survival, a much higher and more rewarding life awaits you.

It's hard to imagine such a positive state of mind when you're locked inside a box of concrete and steel, but it is both real and achievable. You *can* triumph over the past – over fear, guilt, emptiness, sorrow, dependency, and behavior that hurts yourself and others. The success you are seeking is not limited to money, fame, or physical possessions. True success is harder to measure but much more fulfilling. It can bring peace of mind, dignity, pride, comfort, security, a sense of purpose and achievement, a feeling of connection to the people around you, and a chance to make a useful contribution to the world.

After years in the belly of a prison, you may not believe such success is possible. But I assure you, it IS! And the purpose of this book is to help you achieve it. *99 Days and A Get Up* offers a path an ex-con can follow to a life of security, achievement, and pride. Use it well – now and in the streets – as a guide to a richer, more rewarding future.

After release you must expect to face many periods of stress, trial, and frustration. If you've been down this road before, you know how easy it is to get lost and discouraged. At times, you may wonder why you should bother to go on. Why should you keep trying, through so much hardship, rejection, and hopelessness? At such moments, I want you to flash back on this book. Recall that there is a wealth of beauty and wonder within your grasp – and this is true for every man, woman, and child who has watched the sun set over rows of razor wire.

Nothing here is magic. But if you base your future freedom on these truths – instead of on false hopes and trial and error – you'll improve your chances for survival and success a thousand fold. And while it will never be easy, simple, or quick, *I promise you it can be done!!* Success will require courage, strength of will, and an absolute commitment to be the best you can be. I know of no task that is more demanding but, at the same time, more exciting and rewarding.

In short, life IS worth living, no matter how much adversity you have to overcome. Although your progress may be painfully slow and difficult, be assured of three absolute truths:

1. a quality life is achievable,
2. it is worth the price that must be paid,
3. and YOU can do it!

Now, get up and make it happen!!

FIRST

for prisoners facing release ...

Entering the Home Stretch

■ *Adjusting In, Adjusting Out*

"Soon I will be free – free of fear and humiliation, free to laugh and love, to make a contribution to those I value – free to be private and enjoy a beautiful day – above all, free to be at peace."

Prisons are giant public dumpsters where society throws people defined as "social trash." They are filthy, hurtful places where daily life is sick, twisted, and unspeakably sad. No one was born knowing how to cope with such a negative experience or how to recover from it. Without preparation, a prisoner faces an endless series of dangers and disappointments, both during and after captivity.

The information in this book is written for prisoners facing release. It can help you strengthen your ability to control your fate in the free world and thus improve your chances for survival and success. Understand and use it for what it is: *a roadmap*. The more you review and think about it, the more you will improve your odds of getting up and getting over.

For all prisoners, no matter who they are or how much time they've done, one goal outshines all others: *to get the hell OUT!* After release, the concern shifts to *staying out.* This sounds simple, but for over half of all men and women released from prison, the pain and agony of captivity isn't over ... it will come again!

The question is: how will *you* be one of those who *win* – who remain free and build a rewarding life? How are you going to beat the odds and never, ever come back? The first two years after release represent a long, hard, complicated journey, testing your endurance, determination, and ability to adapt to new situations. So you must use the last year down to get ready for the first year of upcoming freedom – to prepare mentally and emotionally for the demands and opportunities of a new, exciting adventure.

You may be a lucky one and have it made in terms of the transition back into society. You'll be going home, back to an environment you're familiar with, family, friends, etc. Not that you won't experience some difficulties, but you'll have support to help you weather the storm.

Or you may be one of the majority, one who has little or no family and has lost contact with friends over the years. In fact, if released today, you'd have no place to go and no way to get there. If this describes you, the transition from a cell block back into the mainstream of society will be very difficult, requiring special preparation.

As we begin, stop and think back. Remember when you first arrived in the joint? Recall the shock and the serious mental changes you went through to make the harsh adjustments needed to survive in the World of the Damned. It was not an overnight event or a deliberate path but a blind, gradual process you pursued by sheer necessity. If it was your second time down (or more), you were not as shocked or nearly as vulnerable, but you still had to "get your head off the streets" and deal with the grief of losing your family and freedom.

It was almost like you were sent to outer space and forced to live in a hostile environment, breathing artificial air and facing unknown dangers. It was an alien world, but you learned how to survive there. Now that you are returning from prison, the *community* is the alien environment. To survive, you will have to go through a new series of adjustments, just as severe. In fact, many people find life *after* prison even more demanding than life in prison.

I'm not talking about just the obvious survival issues, like money, employment, housing, and transportation. All this matters, don't get me wrong. But your success depends even more on how you deal with the mental, emotional, and social changes that await you. To succeed, you will need determination and some special skills. In particular, you need to understand the change process and the challenges and opportunities you face when coming out of a joint.

A word of caution: too often inmates and their loved ones buy into the false idea that only one problem stands between them and happiness – attaining release. But this just isn't true: release is only the midpoint of a much larger experience that begins the day the gavel falls and follows you to the grave! Every moment of captivity must be used to prepare so that personal fulfillment will be the final outcome. It is time to start thinking about who you're going to be once you hit those bricks, how you intend to carry yourself and deal with those around you.

Clearly, being released from prison is no guarantee of success. However, release from prison *does* give you the chance to actively pursue a rich and rewarding future. This is a wonderful change from your current situation. The burden is on *you,* but so is the opportunity to succeed.

■ *Been Down Forever*

"How much time have I done? Well, I was born with a prison number tattooed on my butt and I've only seen 14 months and 17 days of freedom ever since. What does that tell you!?"

The longer a person is down, the greater the danger that his or her world will shrink to the exact size of a prison compound! This is totally natural, a way to adapt in order to survive. After five years of captivity, most people are so mentally isolated from the community that the free world is more a distorted memory than a fact. After ten years, they may get so tired and empty that they forget any other world actually exists. Prison has become their primary reality.

Many long-term inmates simply don't want to know what's happening out in the world. It hurts too much to be reminded of it when they can't be a part of it. So they withdraw ... just turn their back on life in the streets and build a nest right where they are. While this may be a very reasonable way to cope with long-term absence from the world, you can quickly see the huge gap it creates when it's time to come home.

Others try to stay connected with the world, especially when they get close to release, by keeping informed about current events through TV, magazines, and news from home. But this has pitfalls, too. Although you may start with the facts, much of what you end up with is a twisted picture of the world – a combination of someone else's viewpoint coupled with your own wishful thinking.

Clearly, long termers go through some heavy changes as they get ready to re-enter the land of the living. For many, the hardest part is maintaining faith that they can, in fact, survive and prosper out there in the great unknown. In case you get caught in this trap, let me assure you that the whole notion of your success after release is not an illusion or cruelty joke. It is a true and factual possibility which, with the right understanding and determination,

you can and will achieve!

One of the greatest problems in returning to the community is CHANGE. Never in human history has civilization moved so fast ... but not in prison! The longer you've been locked up, the more radical the changes you will face upon release. So it's important to do all you can to get ready. Don't hide within the prison setting you've grown so used to. Refuse to retreat into the confines of your own mind and daily habits.

You must realize that things out in the world will be different from what you think they will or ought to be. Don't let this stress you out. Although reality is bound to be different from your expectations, you don't have to be overwhelmed by it. As with all aspects of life, your existence after prison will be both good and bad. What you must remember is that, even with all its dangers and difficulties, the world is also a place of great beauty and wonder!

As you get close to the door, identify the invisible chains that bind you and begin to cut yourself loose in a slow and orderly manner. To best prepare for the streets, you must examine your values and feelings: those that got you into prison as well as those you have collected while inside. Decide which of them were negative and destructive, and define something positive to take their place. You will also find that you have gained useful insights from facing adversity; examine those, too, and prepare to apply this hard-won knowledge in constructive ways.

If you have been in prison so long you feel like you were born there, begin to wake up from the coma you've been lost in! As we will discuss a little later, sit down and have a

99 DAYS AND A GET UP

serious talk with yourself about the reality of your future. You ARE getting out!! Don't just sit in the TV room trying to ignore it; you *must* begin to collect yourself on every level. If you wait any longer, you will get lost in the panic of short pains and be on the streets before you can get your head or heart right.

If you're leaving after three to five years, the whole trip will feel like rebirth. If you are exiting after seven, ten, fifteen years or more, it IS rebirth! In every case, it brings a tidal wave of excitement mixed with fear, sometimes threatening to drown you just as you are finally attaining your ancient dream of freedom. This is where you need faith and strength ... because you have to keep swimming right through the wave.

Despite the difficulties, be encouraged! The longer you've been away, the greater the rush of release. Admittedly, you will face a lot of confusion and conflicting emotions, but you can and will sort things out. Give yourself time to adjust; just get out there and enjoy the countless little things the squares take for granted. You will be delighted to find how refreshing it is just to take a walk in the rain, to be able to come and go as you please, to experience the joy of privacy. What you are facing is *renewal!!* Don't fear it, *rejoice and embrace it!!*

■ *A-l-m-o-s-t Short!*

"After a couple of bits, you learn that survival is based on the strength of your heart and mind. If you can survive years in the bowels of a prison, you can surely learn to survive in the free world. You have too much living to do to let yourself be consumed again – by anyone, anything, anywhere, anytime."

Some people are so short the day they drive up that they are back on the streets before their fingerprints dry. For most, however, life in the joint involves years of grief, isolation, and regret. For still others, the truly long termers, prison becomes a bottomless pit into which a person pours his or her life force while hoping for a miracle ... one birthday, one Christmas, one fourth of July after another.

All factors considered, "getting short" means different things to different people. On a practical level, a person is close to release when within a year of his or her release date. By then the bust, conviction, loss of loved ones, and adjustment into prison are over and done with. You are living each day pretty much on auto pilot, just the same old jive day in, day out. At this point, you have the mental energy and stability needed to deal with the question: *"Now What?"*

Facing this question forces you to make a firm commitment to yourself and to your intention to build a positive future. Now, obviously you don't *have* to do this ... after all, it is a lot less stressful to stay in a trance and do nothing until they process your release papers. But you really don't want to do that! The streets are dangerous enough. If you don't tighten up your act in advance, you are inviting disaster – and with it, the anguish, sorrow, and shame of being a social reject and slave of the state.

Get one thing straight: "preparation" is far more than trying to figure out where to live, how to get a job and score a used car. It's about attitude and positive ways to carry yourself ... deciding how you are going to deal with people and what values you are going to live by. All this is hard work, involving ten carloads of uncertainty and tension, so it's tempting not to face it. Plus, we as humans tend to put things off – laying back in the daily groove, telling ourselves that everything will be cool, that all we need is OUT! While it may be natural to feel this way, facing the world after years in a cage is an un-natural situation, and extraordinary efforts are required to overcome it.

In fact, *when* you prepare yourself is as critical as *how* you do it. For example, much of the mental preparation for release needs to be done six to nine months before release. Why not wait till you get closer to the door? Because the shorter you get, the more distracted and stressed out you become – and this leaves you without the energy and attention needed for preparation. You have to hit the ground running the day of exit, so now is exactly the right time to begin a deliberate process of self-inventory and reality checks.

While preparation should be an ongoing effort, it doesn't make any sense to get all bent out of shape and crazy behind it. Don't obsess over the moment of release; just spend an hour a day inside your head, taking an open and honest look at yourself. Not some outlaw or hard-ass image you've gotten off into – but what you truly are in your center and what kind of person you aspire to be. Look within yourself for answers to such questions as:

What am I going to be and do in the future that is a true improvement over my past attitude and actions, the things that resulted in my being locked down like a mad dog?

How can I best take control of my fate so that I am truly 'in charge' of what happens to me??

What must I do to 'make amends,' both to myself and to others, for the grief and discomfort my actions have caused?

What is really worth living for ... and what am I willing to do to achieve it? What price am I willing to pay ... and for how long??

Your answers hold the key to true freedom. Freedom from past influences and events. Freedom from the chains of fear, rage, longing, and isolation. Freedom from forces outside yourself that seem to control your mind and spirit.

Exploring your inner self is hard work, but well worth the effort. Your purpose is to *connect* with yourself, with who you are and wish to become. Through this process, you gain a growing sense of your center, your real identity as a person of worth. Only from that level of deep awareness can you really connect with the people you love and value and, ultimately, with anyone you meet in the free world.

Harsh though it has been, your imprisonment is a "learning tool." You can use the power and insight gained from the experience as fuel for your progress and growth. The sooner you consciously apply it that way, the smoother your re-entry to the free world will be. And so, use THIS very moment for serious review and reflection. Do it now, before you get caught up and distracted in the rush for the door.

Getting Ready for the World

▨ *180 Days and Counting*

"Six months from the door the dawn begins to break – they may actually let you out of here! But it's a confusing time: you are too short to ignore it but still not close enough to believe it!"

Just when you are sure that nothing can be harder than life in prison, you snap to the fact that you'll soon be crudely evicted – back into the free world where the *real* challenge begins! In fact, release is not the end of your ordeal. It is just *the next step* in a long, cold-blooded journey that begins at sentencing and doesn't truly end until you die.

A prisoner nearing release faces a crossroads. One road is long and steep, leading to hard-won accomplishment, dignity, and pride. The other is short, offering only another round of heart-breaking failure as a slave of the criminal justice system and your own internal demons.

I assume that you are sick to the bone of living in fruitless captivity, thinking of yourself as a social outcast. You know by now that being locked up like a monkey in a zoo has only one purpose – *to learn enough to get out and to stay out.* Sitting in a TV room, running a jail house hustle, or playing dominos will NOT get you ready to succeed after release. Nor will being caught up in the prison rat race, gang activities, or surrendering to anger, self-pity, or romantic illusions of how easy things will be.

During the first few years after your return to the mad, mean world, you will have to stay focused and motivated just to outrun the alligators ... because they are always hungry! Things move fast in the streets. The demands of daily living for the first two years won't give you much chance to stop and sort out who you are and where you're going. This means that your fate will be strongly influenced by what you do *right here and now.*

I don't mean you should find a job, start a business, or build a bank roll from inside a cell. Those tasks are usually not possible while you're locked up. No, I'm talking about repairing and improving the ways you think and how you react to yourself and the things that go down around you.

It would be a lot easier to take a nap or write a letter home than to examine your own values and actions. But you are going to be reborn to the world sometime in the next six months, and you have a lot of internal housekeeping to do. This means looking deep inside yourself, taking an honest inventory, and making every effort to fix whatever doesn't work. No one can, will, or should do this for you: it is your right and your responsibility. In fact, it is the key to true freedom.

▪ *Find a Quiet Spot*

"Prisons are tiny places where everyone watches everyone else. A prisoner's greatest treasure is PRIVACY – which only exists inside your mind. To be private, you must intentionally make the journey inward to your Center."

To begin, go find someplace to hide and think! Try the library, the corner of the rec yard, or perhaps the chapel when no one is around. If nothing else, use the times you cannot sleep at 3 a.m. to define your future. Remember that your goal is to be positive and constructive, not negative and disruptive. So don't obsess over anything and get all stressed out. Instead, spend fifteen minutes just being quiet, breathing deeply and balancing your emotions, letting your thoughts settle down. Then begin to reflect ....

Look at where your head was when you first rolled in off the streets. Examine the wealth of changes you've gone through, both good and bad, as you've adapted to the vile nature of your setting. Reflect on your attitude toward yourself and others. How have your views and values changed? Surely they have, but how?

Are you any wiser ... or just wilder? What have you learned about yourself and human nature? Have you realized yet that everything that happens has a cause ... and that by controlling your actions

you can better control your future? Most of all, have you accepted responsibility for *your* role in the circus of errors that lead to your imprisonment?

LOOK, *really look,* deep into your basic nature – that "meeting place" where all the different parts of who and what you are come together. As with all human beings, you will find a lot of contradictions, but don't duck and dodge. It's a waste of time and enough of that has already occurred. Avoiding the truth only prolongs the grief and delays the relief. And given the heavy changes you face in the free world, the very last thing you can afford to do is deceive yourself!

As you go through this struggle to get honest, it helps to recall that you are doing this important work not for the Man or for your people, but for *yourself.* Not because you have to, but because it will contribute to the quality of your daily life. Your goal is to discover a path leading to maximum freedom and success, thus freeing yourself from the multitude of forces which enslave you. So set aside the pre-recorded jive and destructive games, and take a truthful look at the thoughts and feelings that drive you.

As the contents of your mind parade by, you will realize that you have amassed an assortment of thoughts to help justify and sustain your behavior. Examine them to see if it is in your best interest to keep them or to flush them. Many are simply random chunks of experience you collected and held on to. Now is the time to review them and decide what will be useful as you go forward into the world.

Chances are you will find a lot of emotional garbage: anger, denial, self-pity, lame excuses, blind dependencies, false identities, and useless defenses, just to name a few. Don't get lost in what's "good" or "bad." Instead focus on the *results* of your behavior and how you feel deep within yourself afterwards. What impact do your usual responses and knee jerk reactions have on yourself and on others?

A lot of what you discover will be things you brought with you from the streets ... stuff that has collected since childhood. Much of this is very old and deep-seated; as such it is the hardest to confront and change. You will also find attitudes and actions you picked up in the pen, born of an out-house lifestyle. But no matter what the source, this is the ideal time to take stock of who and what you are. What are you *really* made of? Are you a decent person or a manipulative predator – or a little of both? Even more, what do you want to be? And are you willing to stand up and take positive control of your values and actions?

Through this inventory process, you sort out the useful from the trash, the real from the false. As you go along, take special note of the thoughts, feelings, and actions that consistently result in pain, shame, dishonor, anxiety, guilt, and isolation. Then consider their direct opposites, such as comfort, pride, harmony, forgiveness, peace, and belonging. Study each of these positive elements very closely until you see that you *do* have a choice in most cases!

Practice turning the negatives around a little bit each day, both in your awareness and by actually performing small acts of "positive reversal." Try something new. Where you find fear, practice bravery. Where you find rage, practice forgiveness. Not to do favors for anybody else, but to move beyond the darkness of the past into the light of a positive future. Such efforts may seem too simple to do much good, but if practiced with a deliberate intent to break free from negative habits, they will improve your chances of success by a thousand percent!

▓ *Getting REAL*

"The woman I loved was a jailhouse illusion ... a redheaded phantom that haunted my dreams, promising delights she would never deliver. After they cut me loose, I tried to find her – that's when the real hell began!!"

As you examine and re-define the things that matter to you and the person you want to become, be sure to include an honest look at the goals and ambitions you will carry out with you. Some of the most serious problems faced by all ex-cons and their loved ones come from *illusion* and *false expectations*. As prisoners, our hopes for the future are too often built on what we *wish* life to be rather than what it actually IS. Some of the "visions" we create are real and achievable but many are NOT! And when they are not, it makes us extremely vulnerable to expanded fear, failure, and grief.

Illusion is especially dangerous because it is almost impossible for prisoners to avoid. As we struggle to survive the despair that comes with the whole punishment event, we create mental and emotional pictures to help us maintain a sense of hope. But life in prison is so unnatural and so far removed from life in the community that it distorts our view of reality. After a while, it's hard to tell where reality ends and fantasy begins. A voice inside our heads warns us that we are losing our reason, becoming caught up in jail house madness, but after awhile we don't listen ... or simply don't care.

Every prisoner is haunted by his or her own illusions, by wishes and desires that don't fit reality. If we get lost in our fantasies, we may base all our hopes and plans for the future on things that don't exist outside our own minds. When we walk out of prison and try to build our future freedom on these false expectations, they will blow up like a series of land mines set to explode as soon as we put our weight on them.

It's hard to decide what does more damage: the loss of your illusion ... or the hell you put yourself through to maintain it. The longer you try to hang on and refuse to face reality, the more effort you waste and the harder it will be to recover. If you don't wise up in time, the result can be disaster – the loss of everything you have worked and hoped for. All too often, the resulting rage and disappointment can lead to reckless behavior that will send you right back to the joint. And as the gate slams behind you again, you KNOW the truth: *you did this to yourself!*

The solution, of course, is NOT to base your fate on falsehood, no matter how tempting it may be. But this is easier said than done. On a mental level, you may realize that your visions of the future are not based on reality, but your emotions and your need to hope can blur your judgment. This is one of the chief dangers of addiction or dependency of any kind – because it lies, making promises that it never keeps. It promises to make the pain go away or to bring good feelings, but *it always takes more than it gives!* And in the process, it distorts your thinking so that you don't see what is happening and can't make good decisions to deal with it.

Your success in the free world depends to a large extent on making the right choices. To do so, you need good information – the true facts, not wishful thinking. Above all, you must be honest and real with yourself. It's just fine to have dreams but you must understand the difference between a dream and an illusion: *a dream can be achieved but an illusion cannot!* And after years in the unreal world of prison, it can be extremely hard to tell the difference.

So take time now to examine your expectations of the future. What is your mental picture of the first few months after your release? How do you expect other people to react to you? How do you expect to react yourself? How hard will it be to get back on your feet – to get a job, housing, transportation? How long will it take? What could go wrong?

To develop realistic plans for the future, you need a clear mind and the courage to face reality. You must work constantly to overcome false expectations and distorted thinking. In every case, *illusion is your enemy!!* By doing all you can now to bring your thoughts into line with what is real and true, you will significantly improve your chances of survival and success after release.

■ Owning Yourself

"Personal responsibility is a two-edged sword: you can choose to direct your own fate and live with the results ... or you can hide from responsibility and die a slave. This is the reality we all face! "

There is one essential reality you must grasp when preparing for the free world: *you* are responsible for your own life – past and present, good and bad. For many of us, this is not a pleasant thought. We often refuse to take responsibility for things we have done and events that have happened to us. But this attitude is the kiss of death for a person leaving prison! The reason is simple: if you are not responsible for what happens in your life, then you don't have any control over what awaits you after release.

Once you accept that you are in fact the captain of your own ship, you realize that you have the ability to guide and improve your future by changing the ways you think and act. You do not have to be a slave!!! But it's up to you to take "ownership" of your own life and future. And the price of ownership is that you accept responsibility for who you are, what you do, and the results of your actions. Until you do this, your life doesn't truly belong to you.

This whole concept of self-responsibility, which many of us have always considered a negative burden, is in fact our greatest treasure. Rather than being a chain which binds us with guilt, shame, and punishment, it is actually the source of our freedom. It gives us the power to choose and the opportunity to reap the rewards of positive actions. Without it, everything that happens to us is either blind luck or controlled by someone else.

Being in control of your life does not mean you have control over nature or a lot of the insanity and suffering that comes down. But you do have control over how you respond to events. In short, you always have the ability to choose how you will handle what life throws your way.

So, as you prepare to expand control of your life, I suggest that you make three basic commitments to yourself. First, realize that you are responsible for your choices and your actions ... not just sometimes, but *always*. Second, strive to base everything you think, feel, and do on that which is true, real, and fair. Third, stop and think. Refuse to be controlled by raw emotion; analyze the best way to handle the next step in any given situation.

As you focus on and practice these three things, you will gain greater power and control over your decisions and actions. And this will make your plans for the future far more real and achievable than those blindly composed in a jail-house fantasy.

■ It's Actually Gonna Happen!

"When the realization finally hit me that I was actually going to be released, it felt as if someone had thrown me into a roaring river. I had only two choices – sink like a rock or swim like hell!!"

The sun keeps coming up and going down and finally it starts to sink in that you're going back into the free world. One thing I can assure you is that folks there will not tolerate prison values. Nor will they accept anyone too inflexible to readjust to community standards. Now is the time to confront the mountain of jail-house jive and emotional poison that has collected within you.

Prison, as you well know, is full of traps and a big one is having to take on an "attitude." We have all watched people adapt with different ways of thinking and acting in order to cope with life in a human cesspool. One sad, typical result is that they slowly become a part of the whole pathetic process, just to avoid being eaten alive. This evolution from "shark bait" to "shark" is one of the ultimate traps of having done time.

So how bad is *your* attitude? You may think you're cool, rough and tough and can handle yourself. And this may indeed be true. Certainly these qualities are both valued and necessary for survival in prison. But they won't work for you in the free world. If you put on your mean mask once you're on the streets, people will simply turn and walk (or run) away, leaving you without the things you need and want. Then you find yourself as lonely and cut off as you were in the pen. You have simply relocated your captivity to the streets.

Whether we admit it to ourselves or not, most inmates and ex-inmates have a mountain of rage and fear inside, hidden behind the bad attitude we show to others. So a big part of your success in the free world will depend on how well you come to terms with these thoughts and feel-

ings. If you don't deal with them, the ugliness you carry around inside will pollute your mind and heart, making you sullen and nasty and threatening your chances for future good.

Of course you can't simply flush away all the accumulated poison, especially while still a prisoner. But you can make a lot of progress by including this issue as part of your mental inventory. Become consciously aware of the thoughts and actions you have adopted as part of the prison environment and outlaw lifestyle. Evaluate where they come from and what they lead to, then decide if you want to carry them with you into the free world. Let this process be constantly cooking in the back of your mind as you move toward the door.

Be always on guard to avoid falling prey to a "nasty attitude," especially when you're under a lot of stress. If you walk out the front gate wanting to bite people's faces off, the Man has you beat ... because the odds are high that you'll actually do it and be back!! Learn to exercise self-control. Be careful not to put yourself into situations that are likely to trigger negative, hostile responses. In the free world, just as in the joint, you have to be super careful who you hang with and the situations you get sucked into. This requires constant awareness, so get your emotions and reactions in check. If your attitude is still a problem after you've been out a year, be smart and seek professional help to deal with it.

▌ 60 Moons of Arrest-Free Living

"Ex-cons who remain arrest-free for five years have a 97% chance of staying free forever! THIS is our target ... how do we get there?!!"

When making plans for release, your first concern is survival, right? You have to meet the basic needs required to stay alive. But for a prisoner trying to establish a life after prison, there is another concern just as basic as survival. Consider this: in order to build a life in the free world, you have to actually be *in* the free world. So after you get out of prison, your first major goal must be to stay out. Although this sounds absurdly obvious, it is very hard to do. To achieve it, you must make the right choices at the right times and avoid a long list of possible traps, such as picking up new charges, getting off into domestic strife, or violating some nickel and dime condition of parole.

But isn't there more to life on the streets!?! Surely there HAS to be ... much more. And it's true that staying out is not an end in itself. But it is fundamental to everything else you want to achieve in life. If you don't succeed in staying out, your alternative is to live and die in captivity, with no real possibility of comfort and satisfaction, much less any chance for major change or achievement.

To help you achieve ongoing freedom, I suggest that you set yourself a specific target of staying arrest-free for five years. This target is so essential to your success that, when you look in the mirror, I want you to see the words *Five Years Arrest-Free* tattooed across your forehead! It is your most important long-term concern, and my purpose is to help you achieve it. Everything else that you want or need depends on achieving this vital goal.

But why five years? That's a hell of a long time! I can assure you, after 35 years of observation, that when a person keeps out of trouble that long, there is an excellent chance he or she will stay out forever. To remain out of harm's way for 60 months, you have to learn to live by values that society will accept. This means making a commitment to positive, constructive conduct. You may be able to hide negative, hurtful behavior for quite a while, but the law of averages will not permit you to function arrest-free for five years if you're ripping and running!!

I'm not suggesting that you go underground or move to South America to avoid detection. Nor do I suggest you put on a halo and grow wings. But you do need to learn to live in ways that give you the best odds of remaining arrest-free. Before all else, you must avoid any actions or situations that might make you a target for an arrest warrant!

You don't have to be a saint. But you do have to use good judgment and avoid stupid, silly, destructive acts. Now, I acknowledge upfront that this approach will rule out many strange, dangerous, and exciting things that appeal to risk-taking people. For example, by making a commitment to five years of freedom, robbery is no longer an option, and selling speed to college kids is equally out of the question. And when a group of bros elects to knock off a liquor store, you don't go, not even to drive the getaway car.

I know all this sounds square and painfully boring, but it works. Examples are easy to find. If you don't drink and drive, you won't be busted for DWI. If you're not hanging and banging in a crack house, you're not likely to get swept up in a raid. In short, to reach five years of freedom, you cannot engage in activity that makes you a target for the Man. You see, for ex-cons determined to make a better life, the key is to use your brain!! Refuse to place yourself or anyone else at risk. You don't have to be a genius to figure this one out!

This is especially true for those of us with a serious criminal history, because our past makes us more visible and vulnerable to another fall. This is a cold-blooded fact. So the first rule is, always think before you act. Ask yourself: "If I do this, can it get me stopped, popped, stripped, and shipped?" If the answer is yes, let it go … simply don't do it! There is nothing more to be said. Don't minimize it – don't ignore the truth. Find another option. Make the decision now to NEVER again place yourself in a position to give control of your body to the government – or give power over your mind to any external person, feeling, or thing.

It may sound like I'm telling you to roll over like a trained seal and be happy with the rotten fish that life casts your way. NOT SO! The truth is, in the free world you have a wide variety of choices … a broad array of possible satisfactions and rewards. If you are resourceful, creative, and determined, you can interact with many wonderful people, places, and things – without hurting yourself or anyone else. The good news is that the rewards for a positive, constructive way of life are great and deeply fulfilling.

On the other hand, being locked down like a gorilla in a cage offers zero opportunity for living the good life. There's no glory in playing gangster for ten minutes, then paying for it with a ten-year slice of your life. So once you're back in the world, watch yourself very, very closely. Monitor every thought, feeling, action, and decision in order to protect your freedom and improve your life. Make up your mind to be the master of your own destiny. There are many ways to secure your needs and wants without setting yourself up to be stepped on by the state … again. But, as always, it's your choice – even when you don't think you have any choice at all!

▌ *Meeting Survival Needs*

"Hope for the best, expect the worst, and prepare yourself to adapt to whatever comes your way. You have what it takes, just as long as you refuse to let anyone or anything control your mind or break your heart."

In prison, you have very few choices; every day is the same old dull routine. But in the free world, just the opposite is true. Instead of having too few things to do, you have too many … and they often compete with each other. So you have to make constant adjustments and decisions about how to apply your time and energy.

Clearly, you need to be ready to roll when you hit the bricks in order to survive and prosper in daily life. There won't be much time to lay back and think things through. You need a plan to help you organize and focus on your most important goals.

In fact, it's smart to develop two types of plans to guide you after release. The first is often called "survival" or "short-range" because it deals with the minimum requirements you must have to exist ... *the here and now*. The second type – a "quality of life" or "long-range" plan – deals with a broader range of issues (like learning a new trade or having children) that you hope to achieve in the future.

In this section, we will talk about your survival plan because it is most immediate to your needs. It will include the information you would put into an institutional parole or release plan, if you are required to have one. We will discuss quality of life planning later, in the section on life after release, as you think about moving beyond mere survival.

A useful survival plan must, above all, be *practical and achievable!* As we have discussed, most prisoners construct a plan during captivity based on wishful thinking, only to run into setbacks and frustration when reality hits. To reduce this problem, be honest with yourself about your expectations. Then find ways to check them against reality.

You may be able to do some checking yourself if you have access to a library or newspapers. But if at all possible, you need to do reality checks with free world people who have their heads screwed on straight. This is useful both before and after release. And if someone you trust and respect suggests that your plans may not work out as you hope, take heed! Don't ignore them or get discouraged ... just the opposite, *listen closely and adapt quickly.*

An important part of planning is to prepare for the unexpected. You can't have a plan that covers every possibility, but always keep in mind that things may not work out the way you expect. Think about what will happen if something you were counting on doesn't come through. Have some ideas for a back-up plan in case this happens, and be prepared to revise your plans quickly and often.

A survival plan covers some basic needs:

1. a survival budget and source of essential funds
2. employment
3. family and personal support
4. housing
5. transportation
6. health care
7. legal concerns and supervision
8. recreation
9. personal growth
10. spiritual nourishment and growth

But how, you may ask, can a prisoner do useful planning from inside a joint?? You can perform the first two essential stages of effective planning: organization and information gathering. Start by identifying your needs in each area noted above. Focus on the time right after release and think it through carefully, day by day and step by step. As you picture what might happen, you may see more needs and problems ahead than you had expected. That sounds bad, but really it's good. You haven't created any new problems. You would have run into them anyway, but now you have a chance to get ready.

Once you have a list of needs, look for ways to meet each one. You may be able to get written information about resources and programs that offer help, perhaps by writing to agencies yourself or asking your family to inquire. Simply having such information doesn't fix anything, but it will certainly improve the odds of meeting your needs once released.

Survival plans are most useful when combined with an *action plan* that includes dates, times, and tasks – what you intend to do to achieve your immediate goals. It sounds simple enough to go home, relax, see your family and friends, then find a job. But in all the rush of activity and emotion, you may find your plans getting lost or confused. If you have an action plan, especially for the first few days and weeks of freedom, it will help you focus on what you need to do next.

Study the following review of survival needs and pursue creative ways to get as much practical knowledge as possible. Then dedicate serious time and attention to making a list of basic steps that you will follow to take care of business the first few weeks or months after release. As you learn more, you can revise and update your plans.

Keep it simple; don't overload yourself in the first few days of freedom. Take care of essentials and leave some time to spend just get-ting used to things and savoring your freedom. By gaining the skills necessary to meet your survival needs, you are setting the stage for greater fulfillment as you move forward toward higher goals.

SURVIVAL BUDGET AND FUNDS

"Money doesn't matter, as long as you've got some! But when you're broke, you can get desperate and do something stupid … DON'T!"

Start by developing a budget – a list of what you will need money for, how much you expect to need for each category, and when you will need it. Budgeting is a valuable skill, not just for survival, but to help you achieve your goals throughout life. So make it a habit to update your budget regularly and keep track of how you spend your money.

You may receive some gate money when released; if so, find out how much and think about how far it will take you – maybe no further than the bus ride home! Beware of blowing it by partying or buying new clothes the minute you walk out the gate. If you do, you might never get out of town.

After basic survival needs like food are met, a major concern is start up costs like deposits (apartment, utilities, telephone, etc.), work clothes and tools, and basic transportation. Try to postpone as many of these costs as you can for the first 90 days, until you get some cash flow going. This might include planning to stay with family or in a halfway house until you get on your feet. Use three months as a reasonable goal to be able to go out on your own.

The ideal situation is to have a nest egg that can cover you for up to the first three months after release. Although very few can do this, be thinking of any legal and ethical way to have something waiting for you, no matter how little it may be. Even if it's not much, something is always better than nothing.

EMPLOYMENT

"Employment after prison?? Actually it's pretty simple – you take the first crappy job you can find and be steady looking for something better."

Work, deal, or steal: those are your basic options. Dealing and stealing are quick tickets back to the pen. So, of all your needs fresh out of prison, finding a job is at the top of the list. Employment for an ex-con is a major topic by itself, so I strongly advise you to get a copy of the book *Man, I Need a Job!* (published by OPEN, INC., see the back of this book for information) and use it to prepare yourself to handle this critical issue. It will also help for your family or loved ones to read it in order to understand what you are facing and how to support your efforts.

Caution: don't make your stress any worse by thinking that you must find a job before you get out. Sometimes this is possible with employers who knew you on the streets, but typically no business man with any sense hires someone on the blind. Plus, without actually being on site you don't know what's real and what's not. So, while it is encouraging to have a strong prospect, don't base your fate on having a solid job offer in advance of exit. Even if you do have a job promised, circumstances can change quickly and the job may not be there when you get out. What is valuable and useful, however, is *a firm promise of an interview!!* So do everything you can to get an opportunity to sit down with a potential employer face to face as soon as you can.

By the law of averages, you will probably have to apply for ten jobs before you get one good job offer. You may need to work as temporary labor for awhile to get survival funds until you find a permanent job and get a cash flow started. But don't get discouraged. Set your mind now to follow this formula and don't give up. The longer you keep trying, the more the odds will turn in your favor.

FAMILY AND PERSONAL SUPPORT

"Just like in the joint, the few people who care about you are your greatest treasure. Treat them like gold – but be very selective and don't hesitate to avoid anyone who might threaten your freedom."

Family, loved ones, friends, and associates all combine to become your "support system." As you know, this is your main link to the world, both in and out of prison, and the source of comfort, encouragement, and help when needed. Since family and loved ones are so important, we will discuss your relationship with them in later sections.

But many prisoners don't have family or their family ties have been broken by imprisonment and the events that led up to it. If this describes your situation, you may benefit by developing a new personal support system. I'm not talking about getting a pen pal or persuading your cell partner's old lady's girl friend to visit you. Although not always the case, these relationships are often based on fantasy and don't work out after release. But you may be able to find someone – maybe a chaplain, teacher, counselor, or volunteer – who is willing to help you get good information and give you realistic feedback on your plans for the future.

In return for this person's help, you owe him or her honesty, appreciation, and respect. Always keep in mind what is reasonable for you to request – including what is allowed by prison regulations – and don't expect this person to carry you. Once you are in the community, it is smart to seek a similar advisor who can offer guidance, encouragement, and a dose of reality to test your plans. Whenever someone gives you this type of support, show your appreciation by making good use of their advice and never abusing their trust.

Nothing is more critical to your fate than the quality of your relationships, so think about who you are (and who you are not) going to relate to in the streets and the best ways to do it. Most of us have only a few relationships still intact when we get out of prison and it is natural to hang with them ... but be careful. One obvious suggestion: stay close to those who are solid, *but cut all the fools loose!* You know the difference. If someone is generating more heat than a floor furnace, avoid them like the plague or you will get caught in the very same net they do. Better to be lonely in the streets than locked up with a bunch of home boys.

HOUSING

"Waking up in a bleak little room can be depressing as hell, but it's only a temporary condition. Remind yourself that you are only passing through, just moving on to a better place."

Finding a place to live should always be a major part of a prisoner's release plan. People often intend to return to family, but if that option is not available, you must make other plans. One alternative – in some cases a requirement – is a halfway house. Although this may not seem like an appealing option (we will discuss some concerns about staying in a halfway house in the second section of this book), it does provide two of life's essentials – food and shelter – so don't reject it out of hand. If you can't get a bed at a halfway house, you can check into other types of shelters, which are supported by nonprofit and faith-based organizations in most cities.

Although halfway houses and shelters are not the ideal living situation, they sure beat a prison cell or sleeping under a bridge. They may also help with other needs such as finding a job, so appreciate and use them for what they offer. While staying there, you can sometimes save until you have enough money for apartment rent, utilities, and deposits. Try to put away enough savings to cover an extra two to three months living expenses before you make the move. This helps because when you're getting started, it just takes one ill wind to blow down your whole house of cards.

Be aware that new laws and policies have been adopted in many places to limit ex-convicts' access to public housing because of their criminal and drug history. And many apartment owners have started doing background checks, including criminal history checks, on prospective tenants. Whether this is fair or right is not the issue; what does matter is that you find ways to overcome such obstacles in your path as you strive to rebuild your life.

This is also a grave concern for inmates' families, who can be evicted if their landlord learns they are keeping an ex-con under their roof. Trying to hide this fact doesn't solve the problem because a neighbor or government employee can give you away, either intentionally or not. So if you do move back into an apartment with your family, keep a low profile and don't do anything that might stir up trouble.

It's hard to avoid this problem because information about your criminal record can easily be discovered through computers, the Internet, and people who do criminal history checks for a living. So learn what types of housing restrictions apply in the community where you plan to live. If you know in advance, it won't be such a shock when you run into it and you will have time to figure out how to handle it. Do your best not to get discouraged and let this kind of trash bend you out of shape or push you into an act of desperation or rage. Just be aware that such problems exist so you can be mentally and emotionally prepared.

TRANSPORTATION

"Your goal is a car that actually runs ... until then, you do whatever it takes to get where you need to go. Keep your life simple and operate within your limits. This way your self-reliance will increase, along with your resources."

Unless you plan to stay in the community where you are released, transportation will probably be the first need you run into after release. If you don't have a family member or friend to meet you, you will be using public transportation, most likely a bus. Try to find out the fare and schedule for where you need to go. The schedule is important to be sure you don't get stranded at a bus station or street corner in the middle of the night.

After this immediate need is met, most of us will want a car right away. Having a dependable way to get around is very important, but seldom possible for people fresh out of a joint. Until you can save enough money for a used car, you will need to use public transportation. Today most major urban areas have buses and other forms of mass transit. Get a free schedule of the routes so you can plan ahead to get where you need to be on time. If possible, select a place to live that is on a major bus or public transit route, and look for work near your residence or with easy access by public transit.

Although public transportation is less expensive than a car, you may be shocked to find how much it costs. Sometimes community agencies provide discount or free passes for people in dire need. If you are going out to a halfway house or seeking help through an agency or church, ask in advance if they offer this kind of help.

HEALTH CARE

"Fresh out of prison we tend to ignore our health until a crisis comes along – then we are in serious trouble! Be AWARE of what you do to and with your body. Give it a lot of respect, even if you can't give yourself a lot of attention and care."

Good health is a treasure. It affects everything you do, including your ability to prosper and enjoy your freedom. So learn how to protect and improve your health. Good nutrition, exercise, and rest are important elements. They will also keep you mentally clear and physically fit to deal with problems and overcome the stress that accompanies release.

If you have a health problem (physical or mental) that will need attention when you return to the community, now is the time to research available help and forms of financial support. If you need regular medication, such as for diabetes, AIDS, TB, Hepatitis C, or an emotional illness, try to get a supply to take out with you that will last until you can make arrangements to get a prescription filled after release. If you can't get an appointment with a free-world doctor right away, look for a public health clinic or hospital that may offer the help you need.

Beware of celebrating your release with alcohol or drugs. Not only is it bad for your health, it's bad for your freedom. After the loss of years of your life and the suffering of imprisonment, it's easy to tell yourself that you deserve to "get loose." And the pressure of returning to the streets can drive you to seek escape, so it's an easy trap to fall into. But beware: it is often a quick ticket back to the joint, before you've even gotten your feet on the ground in the free world.

Caution!! If you rolled into the pen under the control of an addiction – drugs, love, booze, sex, gambling, etc. – that very dragon (or one of its cousins) is still out there waiting for a chance to pounce on you. The power of your addiction to dominate you will have a major impact on your mental and emotional condition the day of release. The last thing an ex-con needs is to be owned by anything or anyone! So NOW is the time to give this very serious attention, especially if you have denied the reality of your dependency until now.

If you are already committed to overcoming one or more addictions, this is an equally good time to strengthen your resolve and decide how you will maintain your recovery after release. For persons in active recovery, plan to jump right into a 12-Step program; it's free and provides much needed support.

To learn more about confronting addiction of all types, get a copy of OPEN's book *Life Without a Crutch* (see the back of this book for information) as a valuable aid in your preparation for the world. It deals with regaining control of your life from any addictive behavior, which is essential to success after prison.

LEGAL CONCERNS AND PAROLE

"As a former felon, you have a much higher risk of being arrested than the average citizen. Never get careless and start thinking it's over – because it's never over. So stay alert – when you snooze, you lose!!"

Most people exit prison on some kind of supervision, be it parole, federal probation, electronic monitoring, etc. Some may be required to stay in a halfway house or participate in activities such as counseling. Many also owe restitution or fines or have to pay supervision fees or back child support. And if you have a drug history, expect to be drug tested often and always when you least expect it. It helps to learn in advance the rules you will have to follow. As too many find out, messing up while under supervision can be another fast track back to the joint. So stay on your toes!

You will probably be required to report to your probation or parole officer very soon after release. Be sure you know when and where, and make plans for how you will get there on time. There's no point in being labeled an absconder just because you got lost or didn't have bus fare. We will discuss your relationship with your P.O. in the second section of this book.

If you're not under supervision, congratulations. But that doesn't mean you are home free. Even if you don't have post-release supervision or after you have completed it, your felony history will stay with you, hiding in a computer database waiting to jump up and bite you when you least expect it. Run a tight ship and never forget that your criminal record makes you vulnerable to

future problems. Part of your preparation must include what to do when your past suddenly threatens to consume your future ... because I can assure you it will happen!

RECREATION

"You need to have a good time and that's cool ... just don't do anything that hurts you or someone else. No rush in the world is worth going back to the joint for! I promise you – NONE!"

It may seem dumb to think about having a good time when you are struggling to survive right out of prison, but the fact is you need something simple, cheap, and fun to lighten up what is often a dull, difficult, and dangerous period. Think about something safe and relaxing that you would like to do a few hours a week and plan to make it a part of your life as soon as possible after exit.

Even if you don't take up a formal activity or hobby, find something pleasant and rewarding that keeps you away from the TV. You don't want to leave one tiny, restricted existence and move right back into another one! Some simple form of recreation will help keep you balanced, reduce your stress, and help you focus on your goal of success.

PERSONAL DEVELOPMENT

"The only way to 'beat the system' is to outgrow it!! And the best way to make life meaningful is to be in a constant state of positive change. But you can't sit back and wait, you have to make it happen!!"

One of the really great things about the free world is that it offers so many ways to make your life richer and fuller. Many kinds of education and training opportunities are available in most areas. For those who get tired of flipping burgers, nothing is better than taking some vocational training to expand their skills and income. Learning also brings fresh energy and greater self-respect, which for an ex-con are valuable in themselves.

So check out what is available in the area you release to; costs are often far less than you might expect. You may not be able to get involved in this type of self-advancement right after release; it is something to work on as a more long-term goal. But knowing the possibility is there will give you something to look forward to and remind you of the positive rewards for your hard work.

SPIRITUAL NOURISHMENT AND GROWTH

"The only thing we bring with us at birth and take with us at death is our spiritual essence. Everything else ends up in a Saturday morning garage sale. And I do mean EVERYTHING!"

This is an issue that means very different things to different people. For some it means participating in a specific religious faith system, while others view it as tapping into their higher power or sense of spiritual awareness. No matter what, it is the most private and powerful aspect of us all and one which can have a major influence on our values and actions.

I'm not recommending that you lay back and wait for God to solve all your problems with no effort on your part. But I urge you to maintain a strong connection with this deepest and most meaningful aspect of human nature. If you have the will to do so, plan to continue and strengthen the growth of your spiritual self.

Keeping It Together

◾ *"Short Enough to Fit in a Matchbox!"*

"How do you know when you are finally short? When the smell of freedom is so strong it wakes you up in the middle of the night!"

Well, it's finally around the corner! Unless someone drops a fresh detainer on you or you die in your sleep, you're going to be released within the next 90 days or so. You may be going out on some level of supervision, to a halfway house, or perhaps discharging your sentence. However you hit the bricks, it's difficult to say just how this whole human zoo trip will affect you. The impact of doing time is relative to many factors, including each individual's capacity to adjust to major changes in his or her values and life style.

I can tell you, if you have not

experienced it, that getting short can be a truly difficult and crazy time. With each day that passes, you become just a little more aware and concerned about your upcoming shift out of prison into the harsh demands of the community. This presents a lot of internal conflict: you are delighted to be leaving but equally worried and confused about what the future holds. Once you are down to 90 days or less, the resulting stress gets severe, seeming to reach into every thought and action. And the closer you get, the slower time runs – until the last few weeks when it damn well QUITS!

For some, coming down with a case of gate fever is no big deal. For others, it can become a major catastrophe that pulls them in a dozen parts and even puts their release in peril. No matter what, it is fair to say that every inmate at this stage is influenced by the growing sense of tension and uncertainty ... some very heavy times.

As you well know, prison is a super strange place where *nothing makes sense*. This is especially true when it comes to getting short! Rather than others wishing you well as you get close to the door, what you'll encounter when you reach that magical 90-day period is the petty jealousies and cruelties of the other cons and staff members.

What were once friendly or at least decent relationships suddenly turn sour. Everyday trivial conversations ("Man, when I get outta here, I'm gonna....") are suddenly *out of place*. You actually begin to feel embarrassed about your short-time status. Your new position as a "short-timer" suddenly appears to be at the bottom of everyone else's difficulties. You're getting out but they're not ... and it's all *your* fault that they are so miserable. Very crazy stuff!

■ *It Hurts So Good*

"Fear and stress expand as you approach your kick-out date. Trying to ignore or deny it just makes it worse – better to acknowledge the pressure openly and focus on keeping everything under control. After all, it's not the end of the world ... IT'S THE BEGINNING!!"

It's essential that you be aware of some of the heavy changes both you and your loved ones face before and after release. The following are a few of the critical issues that influence this period of change. These are not in any particular order and the influence of each item will vary according to a person's unique situation and coping abilities, but most will experience some degree of these mental and emotional feelings.

The closer you come to the day of release, the more aware you may be of how *vulnerable* you are going to be back in the world. This creates a great deal of *stress* and *fear* which most people cannot or do not openly express to themselves or others. With all this comes increasing anticipation and *excitement* as you plan for the future. As a result, you will find it hard to believe that the idea of freedom after prison can be so stressful.

All this leads to unexpected attacks of panic and intense uncertainty about what the future actually holds for you. "Can I ... will I ... make it out there? Can I get a job?

How do I tell people about my criminal history ... or should I tell them at all?!" These are just a few of the questions and concerns you may worry about.

Then there are the age-old demons, superstition and paranoia, that lurk in your soul telling you that this place will never let you go, and that everyone is somehow conspiring to screw up your release. Such feelings, real or not, add to your emotional burdens, further expanding your stress level. The typical way most inmates deal with all this is to quietly withdraw into themselves to prepare for release. However, this can isolate you, often causing *breakdowns in communication* with those around you and loved ones on the outside.

At the same time, loved ones are having a very similar, almost parallel experience. They are wondering about the future, too, especially if they've been used and abused in the past and are *still* wondering if you're worth all the trouble you've caused them. Most of all, they worry about what kind of chaos you are going to create when you roll up to the house. Tension and fear within the family may be at an all-time high, and this adds to your *overall sense of distress.*

Consider all these effects as *traps to be avoided* and seek safe, creative ways to reduce the pressure you feel. This will help you stay alert and improve your ability to manage them. When you do stumble into one, see it as a natural sign of getting short and work to get yourself through it with a minimum of damage to yourself and loved ones.

■ *Stay Calm as a Clam*

"This is a high tension time. It's as if the whole joint is conspiring to prevent your release – and they probably ARE!! So stay ultra cool, calm, and collected."

We know that getting short stirs up a mental and emotional hornet's nest. And the shorter a person gets, the more stress builds up and the crazier he or she can become. So be prepared for it and don't let nervous tension turn your world upside down!

Granted there will be a lot of sleepless nights, difficulty eating, and not being able to concentrate for more than ten seconds at a time. But, in a strange way, all this is *normal* for both you and your loved ones. Such distress always comes when someone faces major uncertainty. Understand your feelings for what they are, the natural anxiety and stress that always come with heavy changes. Just concentrate on ways to handle them and mentally refuse to be overwhelmed!

As tension increases, a lot of senseless arguments and hostility can pop up for what seems like no reason. You really want to stay on top of this so it doesn't upset your ability to ease out the gate. Nor do you want to strain your already fragile relationship with your loved ones. This is no time to get sideways with the people who have the greatest concern for your welfare and stand to provide the most help to you during your transition into the free world.

It is vital for you to relax and practice super-human patience and control right now. Spend extra time on the yard, walk a lot, exercise often, write long letters, and do a lot of deep breathing. Also, the tension you and your loved ones feel can be significantly reduced by *sharing* dreams, hopes, fears, and positive expectations with one another. There is a lot of pressure on you and them now. Trying to hide or to deny it's there is deadly.

More than ever before, this is really a time to be honest and humble. Ask your loved ones for advice and support; talk with them. Even though they will never fully understand what you're going through, they often know a lot more about fear and constant worry than you give them credit for. Plus, by knowing where you stand with things and helping you stay in control, their tension will be reduced as well.

Above all, *strive to stay as calm as a clam.* Know in your heart that you will get out and succeed, no matter what adversity you must overcome, now and down the road.

■ *Walk R-e-a-l Light!*

"Now is the time to be the Invisible Man – there, but not there. Above all, keep your mouth shut and avoid eye contact with anyone but yourself in the mirror."

As you move closer and closer to the gate, it seems too good to be true. At this point everyone has the secret fear that something horrible and totally unexpected is going to happen to prevent that all-important release date.

And there's a lot of truth in these feelings. Given the nature of the place, if anything is going to go wrong, it'll probably happen during your last few months in prison. When other inmates realize that you're getting short, they often turn on you due to personal jealousy and spite. Besides, as you have often watched others do when they get close to release, your anxiety level can cause you to run your head and alert the whole population to your pending exit. So, if you're not real careful, you can get off into a trap that you didn't expect.

Above all, *don't panic.* It's essential to stay calm and together. Remind yourself that it's just another day in the Twilight Zone! If you've ever treaded water, now's the time to do so. Take it easy, keep your cool, and walk r-e-a-l light. Don't make any waves, borrow any money, do any drug deals, run up any gambling debts, or piss anybody off. You'll have enough problems with staff and fellow inmates because of your short-time status to keep you busy putting out fires, so move into stealth mode. *Go invisible.*

The best thing to do is simply keep your mouth shut. No need to make the situation worse by waving an "I'm short" flag under anyone's nose. This is just one of the many traps that are so easy to fall into. Think about and avoid them all, because any one of them can cause your downfall. Besides, if you're taking care of business the way you should, there won't be any time left to get off into a trap. Instead, devote every moment to mental and physical preparation for your forthcoming release.

Check it out: as you are getting ready to depart, do not make the typical mistake of mentally leaving prison in advance of your body. All this will do is drive you up a wall and make you vulnerable to the other dangers which lurk all around you. *So while you plan and prepare for the future, keep yourself under control – continue to live in the present.*

At the same time, do not waste another thought or shred of energy on the day-to-day intrigue of prison life. Be watchful but go on *automatic pilot.* Gather your inner strength and resources. Now is the time to focus your total being on preparing for your success in the world. Begin this new chapter in your life by being at the peak of your mental and physical capacities. Stay alert minute by minute. Refuse to let anything disturb your balance or pull you into destructive actions and emotions. When you do get distracted or off into some hassle, practice good damage control and get right back on track.

And Out You Go!

▪ *Moving Forward*

"Prepare to look life right dead in the eye. Have absolute faith that you can survive and prosper."

OK … your kick-out date is around the corner, you're almost there! By now you've thought things out, broken through illusion, overcome many fears, confronted your anger, and made some realistic plans. During this process you've been surprised to discover how much you have learned about yourself and human nature while in prison.

Use your remaining time to separate the good from the bad. List on a piece of paper all the negative trash you brought into the joint or collected while there. Then, the night before you leave, take a match and burn it!! Take out with you only the wisdom and insight you've earned. Be assured that anything real and positive you can do now, as you await that much-desired call to "pack your shit," is for the good!! And the more organized and focused it is, the better off you will be.

Above all, as you get ready to go, train yourself to take a few minutes every week, wherever you are in the world, to purify your mind and heart. This means letting go of a bit more of the filth, grief, and conflicting values that every former prisoner brings home. Use every possible opportunity to look forward rather than back and to focus on what you really want from life. Your future is in the free world and you want to learn how to best fit and function there … so don't refer back to prison life unless you intend to go there!

Remember, the gap between prison and the free world is huge. You can't just push a button behind your ear and suddenly all the changes are in place – that's not real. Instead there will be a process of gradual change, with a series of ups and downs, before you finally feel at home.

Be assured that you have what it takes: not only to cope with life after prison but to replace the whole trip with a deep sense of purpose, achievement, and satisfaction. Make an unbending commitment to yourself that whatever it takes, *you will do it!*

Then, as you watch the sun come

up the day of your release, be proud. First, you survived one of the most demanding experiences of our time and place in history. But above all, you have actually "beaten the system" by extracting personal growth from the nightmare. Permit yourself the rush of that achievement!

■ *What Will the Future Hold?*

"Life on the streets isn't good or bad ... it's BOTH! You have to handle the ups and the downs with an equal faith in the wonder and beauty of life."

Now it's time to actually experience every prisoner's ultimate dream: FREEDOM! What will the future hold for you?

I have found that 80% of what awaits us in the streets depends on our attitude and actions. The world will *always* be both good and bad, so it's our job to seek out the good while we cope with the bad in productive, rewarding ways. What will most influence your future, I believe, is not your skills (although they are important) but your way of seeing yourself and your relationship with the world.

If you view yourself as an outlaw or outcast, you will conduct yourself that way and never become a positive part of the outside world. Having that sense of belonging may not matter to you now, but later it will, as you hunger for greater purpose and satisfaction. If you see the world and everyone in it as your enemy, you will constantly find yourself caught up in some battle that always seems to end in misery, both for you and for others. Equally, if you see

yourself as the powerless victim of a cruel, corrupt society, you will never put forth the courage and determination it takes to make your plans come true.

So as you look forward, hold a mental picture of yourself as a useful, constructive person, respected and valued by yourself and others. Then do everything in your power to make that image real. Hear me: this goal is truly within your reach and worth all the effort it will take to achieve it.

■ *Making Your Future Bright*

"Life after prison is a great adventure! Colors, smells, taste, touch, sound, all so new and powerful ... many as if for the first time. The secret is to take it all in slowly. Savor it ... don't be a glutton!!"

There is so much more to life than the pain and agony of jails and prisons!! In the free world, opportunities exist for personal privacy, for the space and time you need to relate to yourself and those about you. Free people take this opportunity for granted, but for former inmates, privacy is a boundless treasure! It is a big part of what it means to know freedom.

Soon you will be back in the mainstream of the community and once again have the invaluable opportunity to experience a range of joys, from peace and quiet to personal privacy. Mentally prepare to enjoy yourself as you slowly rediscover so many things, big and little, that you'd somehow forgotten. It is possible to feel good about yourself, to enjoy the world around you, and to look forward to each new day.

And it is possible to have rewarding relationships – with the loved ones who stood by you through tough times and with the people you have yet to meet. The encouragement you get from these relationships will help you put the entire crazy prison experience behind you and grow far, far beyond it!!

For you, and for your people, release truly is a rebirth that only comes when you have lost everything and the world stands fresh before you. You are about to have a new start on life – an opportunity that few people have. It is time to let the past go, to hold your head up and face the future with realistic optimism. Be positive and patient and willing to pay your dues ... and you will experience the pride of having survived and moved beyond the chains of the past. Remind yourself, as I do, of something my friend Crazy Frank often said: *"Rollo, if it can get **this** bad, it can get **this** good!"* Thirty-six years later, I can assure you he was right.

SECOND
for ex-prisoners, the day of release ...

■ *Fresh Air!*

"I dream of standing naked under a giant waterfall, washing away years of filth and pain! One way or another, I must get clean!!"

Once you cross the property line and roll beyond sight of the sick, sad place that has been your world for so long, take a deep breath. You will notice how amazingly sweet the air smells ... in fact, everything is fresh and new. Drink it all in and rejoice. Set aside for awhile your concerns about the future and savor this moment that you have dreamed of for so long. Although there will be times when it all seems like "too much," just kick back and enjoy the rush. You deserve it!

So many things that are common place to others are now special and unique for you. As soon as you can, go find a place to watch the sun go down ... in a park, from a hill top, anyplace that is private and safe and quiet. Don't worry that you still feel like a prisoner; that will pass. Just sit under a tree and grant yourself the thrill of newfound liberty – the rebirth of your very existence!

■ *Need Some More Pain??*

"It's like beating your head against a cell wall ... as soon as you quit, you start to feel better IMMEDIATELY! Enough really is enough!!"

Now that you're out, the future depends on *you* – your ability to expand your liberty and remain free forever. As you know, this is not easy.

Prison stripped you of everything you cared about. It confined you against your will in a tiny rectangle of razor wire and grief. Now you've done your bit and been dumped back on the streets. But you know full well that if you aren't careful, you'll get sent back to go through it all over again. Even the guards never really tell you goodbye, *because they expect to see you again!* In fact, if you didn't know better, you might get the idea that prisoners prefer to live in a concrete coffin – if not, why do more than half of us keep going back?!

So it's time to ask yourself some simple questions: "HAVE I HAD ENOUGH?! Is there *anything* in the joint that I need to go back to learn?" If your answer is *"NO!"* – get ready to make some serious changes. It will take courage, determination, and great effort to liberate yourself from the cycle of failure that pulls ex-cons back into the web.

Make the decision right now that you are going to disappoint those who expect you to fail. Instead of looking back at the harsh limits of prison, turn your attention to the future. Let the past go – it is time to focus your total being, body and soul, on building a new life of freedom, security, and achievement.

■ *Everything Has Changed*

"Change is a force of nature, like a wild river rushing down a mountain. And like that river, it threatens to sweep you away until you learn to ride the rapids."

Release is a moment of truth. Suddenly you are evicted and told to get your butt off government property. Now what? First comes the shock of being free again – seeing the stars at night, watching the brightly colored neon lights, the new cars, the traffic jams. To leave a tiny cell or compound where everything moves in slow motion and the next day find yourself in the middle of big-city rush-hour traffic – it can blow your mind! The brightness, speed, and intensity are *overwhelming*. You wonder if you'll ever get used to it. And what about the "good old days"? The people, the places, the events of life before prison ... what happened to them? Did they ever exist, or did you just imagine them?

One thing for sure, things have changed, and I mean drastically. From fashions and fads to politicians, pop music, the price of gas ... nothing is the same – especially you. What about family and friends? They have all changed in many ways, too. In fact, the whole world has changed while you've been down. And the longer you've been away, the more shocking and extreme the change will seem. The world will be far more different and difficult for you if you've done ten years rather than two. And where you did it, in a prison camp or super max, makes a huge difference, too. The longer and more severe your captivity, the longer it will take to reach a point of balance and comfort in the free world.

On the other hand, it seems like some things never change – like debts, taxes, snitches, stress, the pain of rejection, the desire to be loved, and the burdens of everyday living. That's right: some things have changed totally and others *not at all*. What you've got to figure out, and very quickly, is *which is which and what to do about it*.

One very powerful change is the way you will see *yourself* and your place in the world. You will have to answer some questions: "W*ho am I now – good guy or bad guy, decent or vicious, cold or kind? And how should I conduct myself?"* Replacing prison attitudes with free world behavior is confusing and difficult – but it **must** be done. And, like when you walked into the joint, you don't have much time to make the right adjustments if you want to avoid getting chewed up and spit out.

Clearly such powerful changes cannot happen overnight. That's why it is so important to prepare in advance. Continue to have heart-to-heart talks with the "different people" that live inside your head. Put all the jive aside and ask yourself, *"What kind of person do I really want to be? And what must I do each day to make that person real?"* You can do this!! It will take a mountain of motivation and courage, but you *can* make the changes needed to build a rewarding future. Above all, have faith in yourself – your efforts will pay off.

Hear me: change is not a threat to us. We often fear it because it brings uncertainty and stress, but that doesn't mean it's bad. Just the opposite: it's the promise of change that gives us hope for a better future. So set aside your fears and welcome it!

▨ *Not Simple or Easy*

"It's natural to feel overwhelmed at first, but your confidence and control will grow as you slowly rejoin the human race."

It may seem that everyone you meet the first few weeks after your release somehow knows you just got out of prison. It's like you've got a big, red "EX-CON" on your forehead flashing like a neon warning light: "Hey, look at me, I'm a nasty ol' outlaw." Frankly, there is NO truth to such feelings; it's all in your imagination. Most folks are so busy coping with their own daily chores they won't even notice you. So don't make the mistake of assuming that their reaction to you is somehow tied to your past.

Try not to worry about the reactions of others, good or bad. Just keep yourself stable and *very* c-a-l-m. It is completely normal to feel uncomfortable with strangers, in groups, or even with family and friends. Just take it easy and focus on keeping your stress and anxiety under control.

Don't hide from the world out of shame, fear, or embarrassment, or because you don't know what to tell people about yourself or your past. Frankly, having been in jail or prison is just an experience, one of thousands of experiences which people collect during their lives. It's what you are *today* – as reflected in your values and actions – that matters, not where you've been. After you've been out a few years, you will see that your past is no longer the big issue that it was right after release, for you or for others.

In the beginning, however, you will notice concern in people's eyes when they learn of your recent bit in the joint. They will want to know what you went down for, if you hurt anyone, and how you are going to act now. Don't get uptight; this is a reasonable response. Most people won't blindly accept or trust an ex-con, or anyone else for that matter. First they need proof that you are safe and trustworthy. This will take time and steady effort on your part, so keep a good attitude and be willing to pay the price to establish yourself.

Although you can gradually earn people's trust, you can't expect them to understand the adjustments you are going through now. Be careful not to hold that against them or react with resentment or scorn. Remember that you are not alone in experiencing hardship and recovery. *Everyone* has been through hard times in one way or another. Just because theirs didn't arise from the criminal justice system, that doesn't mean they lack understanding or have suffered any less than you.

As you meet people, you may be surprised that you can *see through* the superficial parts of their lives and attitudes – into who and what they really are. As long as you don't let your ego and rage blind you, you will often be able to determine how "real" a person is *very quickly.* This is a skill you had to learn in a jail house to stay alive, both physically and mentally. Now you can put it to more positive use, so respect this ability and it will serve you well.

As you look around at life in the streets, you will find that everyone seems hung up on the trivial details of everyday life. This might bother you because life in prison was filled with get-down survival and the unending quest for freedom. But you must realize that people concentrate on whatever they have to do to keep their lives in order. So don't criticize your family and loved ones for focusing on things which seem to you dull and unimportant.

You may resent it when you have to deal with some of these dull daily tasks yourself. I mean, who gives a damn about the price of milk when you're just three weeks out of Leavenworth? Eventually you will see that it's necessary for everybody – including you – to "take care of business." If you don't look after the small details, they can quickly grow into serious problems. This isn't as dramatic as the struggle to survive in prison, but it is essential for survival in the community. It is one of the many mental adjustments you have to make ... and, gradually, you do.

Remember to take your time dealing with people and the world again. There is no way you can hope to make these adjustments overnight. Life in the free world has its own pace and we cannot control it, no matter how hard we try. Part of your adjustment is learning to recognize

and adapt to the flow. This takes time and patience, so remind yourself to chill out.

A Time for Reunions

■ *Expect the Unexpected*

"It's time to meet a bunch of strangers: some you've never met and others you've known all your life. In either case, you have a mission: to build a relationship based on mutual trust and respect."

Release is a time for reunions, and in most cases they will be stressful for everyone involved. This stress is unavoidable because you've been apart for so long and gone through so many changes. The adjustments will be even harder if you and your loved ones have created a web of illusions and false expectations to help you survive and maintain hope.

You will face people and situations you know very well, but at the same time, they represent total unknowns – so familiar yet totally different! And your loved ones are facing the same situation and feelings. The changes may not be negative, but surely "different" from how things were when you left and how you expected them to be when you came back.

This can be scary and unsettling but you can't let it push you over the edge. Just because reunions may feel "weird," they don't have to be bad or less joyful than you hoped. But you must realize they *will* be different and thus require patience, understanding, and a lot of emotional flexibility.

Expect to feel very low and lost for awhile. You or someone you love may even go through a period of depression, just when you think everyone should be bounding for joy. Don't freak out – this is a predictable part of the experience. It's a natural reaction to the shock when you find things aren't the way you had hoped or expected. All this is normal and will pass as you advance in your dealings with world.

■ *Rebuilding Relationships*

"Your people are wondering who you will really be when you come home. This cannot be answered with mere words, only through actions over time. Strive to be a true friend: honest, sincere, gentle, and dependable. That is what people value above all else."

Only time and consistent effort can reduce the discomfort that naturally comes when people get back together after a long time apart. In one sense you may feel unusually close to your loved ones due to the intensity of your emotions, but in other ways you may be total strangers. The result is a lot of confusion, shock, and frustration, especially when you and your loved one have been "living" for the chance to reunite. Now that you are together, you find that neither of you is the same as you used to be or as you remember each other to be. You *must* allow time to get to know each other all over again. Patience and a good sense of humor will help you get through this period.

As you work to rebuild your relationship, it is important to realize that love is not a magical feeling that just happens to us. It is, before all else, a very special kind of friendship: a positive relationship built on honesty, respect, shared goals, and concern for each other. As with the construction of a fine building, a friendship takes time, patience, and consistency. It grows through commitment and effort; there are no magic buttons you can push. One essential ingredient is communication – being honest and open when you express how you feel and being willing to listen when your friend shares feelings with you. Your sense of comfort and belonging will grow as you develop the trust that is essential for a true friendship.

Every now and then, everyone involved will get impatient, overcome by the sheer burden of trying to build a solid bridge from prison to the community. The real world is not going to fit with all that jive – "oh, baby, baby" and "I've changed, you'll see" – from prison letters and visits. The past is dead. It will take time and work to transform the confusion at the time of release into a rich, rewarding reality. The good news is that life *can* be sweet, especially when you share it with people you love. *Never forget it. Never give up.*

To be successful in building relationships, you must recognize that the world does not revolve around you and your needs. To get a grip on this concept, read the final section of this book, which is written to your family and loved ones. It includes more information about relationships, and it will help you understand what your loved ones have been going through and where their heads are during this difficult time.

▪ Be Kind

"To earn the trust and respect of yourself and others, it's really quite simple: think good thoughts and do good deeds. Anything else is just so much jive."

Your attitude toward yourself and others is the *first thing* people will look for after your release. They want to see who and what you are NOW. Expect them to be cautious and reserved. They will decide how to treat you based on what they sense about your attitude and concern for others. If you frighten them they will run away, so be careful not to put on your "mean mask" just because you're in a bad mood or a bit paranoid.

This requires you to make a major shift from the values of prison, where kindness is considered weakness, to the values of the community where kindness is respected and admired. No one is going to trust you if you use their concern and support as a weapon against them. This change is essential to your efforts to build positive relationships. Keep in mind that simply putting on a nice front won't work if in fact you're a vulture looking for a meal.

Your loved ones want and need to believe in you. But they often have deep-seated concerns about how you're going to handle yourself. You can reduce their stress by not going crazy on anybody and by showing *respect and consideration for others*. Don't get upset and go ballistic if people express doubts about you, directly or indirectly. Remember w*hy* they have these concerns and work even harder to prove that you are

solid. Although it may hurt your feelings, surely you understand why mere words don't relieve their fears. It will take time and steady positive action to rebuild people's trust in you.

During your first few months of freedom, everyone close to you will be under a lot of stress. Be *very* careful to keep your attitude as light and friendly as possible. Your loved ones are counting on you to keep yourself under control, no matter what pressures and problems you have to endure. This is not easy after leaving a joint, so watch yourself very closely. It's not unusual for an ex-con to come home and take out his or her anger on those who least deserve it – just like in a prison visiting room. So keep a close check on how you treat your people, both in what you say and how you say it. If you find that you are unloading your rage or anxiety on the very people that mean the most to you, you must learn a healthy way to reduce the tension in your guts.

To keep stress under control, it helps to admit problems and discuss them openly. If too much pressure builds up and things are about to hit the wall, quietly leave and spend a few hours walking, playing basketball – anything peaceful and positive. Just be careful not to use the situation as an excuse to get crazy, stoned, or violent ... *just don't do it!* If taking a break to let things cool off doesn't work and it looks like physical or mental violence may occur, get professional help to sort things out. Never let any situation come to pain and suffering ... not yours, not theirs.

Beware: use of alcohol and some

drugs (particularly speed) often leads to irrational, out-of-control violence. These chemicals will make you mean and crazy – the very last thing you need when trying to build satisfying relationships after prison. So if you truly want rewarding relationships and a better life, get and stay CLEAN!!!

◼ *New World, New You*

"The hardest thing for an ex-con to do is the very thing we want and need the most ... to be connected with ourselves and others ... to truly be part of the world again ... to share energy, laughter, and love."

One of the greatest losses *anyone* can suffer is losing the ability to feel a deep closeness and concern for another person. And few experiences can do as much harm in this area as life in the belly of a prison. To survive and protect ourselves, we built a barrier around our innermost being. As the years passed, we became distant from ourselves – disconnected from our true feelings and unsure of our place in the world. And as we lost touch with ourselves, we also lost the ability to develop a close connection with others.

Because of this, many ex-cons return home to find we cannot trust or feel close to others, even immediate family and loved ones. People may seem distant or simply "not real" and we don't know why. We may feel cool or detached toward them, unable to feel or unwilling to show any real feeling. This is like living in an emotional solitary cell in our own home, with our own people!

Your goal must be to develop the capacity to love – love in the sense of true concern and honorable intent. But to do this, you must first come to value yourself as a good person, worthy of being loved. Until you can respect and love yourself, you won't have what it takes to respect and love others.

Now that you are out of prison, stop and take a good look at yourself and your ability to love and be loved. If you are a prisoner of your *own* walls, you have truly become a victim of yourself. Your attempt to shield yourself from pain has cut you off from the warmth and tenderness every human being needs.

To love others, you will have to come out from behind the walls you've built over the years to protect yourself from the fools and vultures. This is never easy. In fact, it can be extremely threatening. It requires time and a lot of patience, but it will slowly emerge. Even now, 25 years after my last release, I still find myself feeling "set apart," isolated from others. And this feeling always has great power over me until I admit to myself what is going on and face it directly.

You must stay *constantly* aware of this deadly trap. Work to rebuild your connection to the deepest parts of yourself and to the people you care about. After a few years of conscious effort, if you cannot overcome this isolation on your own, seek professional help to regain your ability to love and show *true* emotion. Refuse to let the past rule you, cutting you off from the wonders of a better day!! Above all, choose the path which leads to a full, rich life.

Survival on the Roller Coaster

▪ A Wild Ride

"It's OK to scream and shout, as long as you hang on and don't jump out! As your control increases, your fears will decrease, and you can enjoy the rush!!"

Release from prison often produces a sense of disorientation which lasts four to twelve weeks. It's like asking yourself, *"Now what?"* and not being able to come up with an answer that makes any sense. Everything is strange and off balance – you can't seem to get your bearings. Just when you thought you'd be regaining control over your life, you are hit with intense feelings of powerlessness and insecurity. Nothing is like it's supposed to be, and you can't figure out what's wrong. Even when things are basically OK, nothing feels right. So it's not unusual to feel lost and overwhelmed.

Unfortunately, the whole punishment trip can leave you emotionally, socially, and spiritually drained and unsure of yourself. This naturally creates a lot of doubt (*"Am I really out!?"*) and feelings of detachment, as though this were happening to someone else and you were watching them live through it. You may experience a *numbness*, as though you are in a dream and not really "of this world." But there are also moments of indefinable joy as you begin to realize that the door actually opened and you have stepped through into the light. Along the way, expect a lot of mood swings – watch them come and watch them go, but don't let any of them possess you.

Next come a few months of mild distress mixed with unexplained fits of depression and a sense of just not belonging, especially in public places and even family gatherings. In fact, you may experience a real problem when you try to be emotionally and physically intimate, as if a wall stands between you and others. If this happens, don't freak out ... it will pass.

At this point everything inside you – your relationship to yourself and to the world – is shifting rapidly, leaving you confused and frustrated. But somehow you know that you can and will handle things as the fog slowly lifts and your vision gradually improves. Expect it to be a strange trip, and keep in mind that this experience is both natural and necessary. Although hard while you're living through it, it is well worth the effort once it's over.

Overall, you can expect the first 24 months to be a cycle of extreme ups and downs. The rush of expanding freedom alternates with times of doubt, difficulty, and confusion. This is the period of maximum stress and danger. In fact, two-thirds of all returns to prison happen in the first two years after release. So work constantly to keep your mental and emotional balance as you watch yourself swing from one extreme to another.

As you begin your third year of freedom, you'll notice the roller coaster is finally slowing down. What a relief! No longer overwhelmed by the demands of sheer survival, you can begin looking for ways to achieve a richer life and greater sense of belonging. It will never be smooth or simple. In fact, it will shift many times from positive to negative and then back again! But don't worry, you're not going crazy. This is simply how it works: for me, for you, for everyone. As time passes, the swings come less often and are less extreme. You can take pride and encouragement from observing your own progress and growth from one year to the next.

■ Invisible Traps

"Focus on staying sane and in control of yourself no matter what – even if you have to do it one minute at a time!"

People fresh out of prison are often shocked to discover that their own feelings and reactions can be as great a threat to their well-being as the prison system ever was. These personal issues aren't as obvious as the obstacles you face in trying to meet your survival needs, but they are just as powerful.

Whether you're a first timer or a seasoned veteran, you will run into these invisible traps. *No one gets to slide on this.* These forces threaten your freedom because they make you less able to cope with the challenges of life in the free world. Each person will respond differently, but there are some basic mental and emotional obstacles all ex-cons face. Be aware of them, but don't be overwhelmed. While they often create major problems, you can reduce their power by understanding and preparing to deal with them.

TRAPS DEALING WITH RELEASE

1. **Shock and confusion**

   A natural response as you shift from the tiny, controlled world of a prison to the fast-paced, demanding nature of the streets.

2. **Intense stress**

   Makes it hard for you to function or even think straight. You may look cool on the outside, but inside you feel like you're ready to explode!

3. **Emotions unstable and hard to control**

   Your moods shift wildly from one extreme to the other. You go to bed calm and confident but awaken all crazy and stressed out. Or you suddenly feel shut out of a group event, when just a few minutes before you were comfortable there.

4. **Short attention span**

   Overloaded by uncertainty and rapid change, it's hard for you to focus on one thought, even for a few seconds. You can't seem to finish anything you start, so you find yourself running around in circles.

5. **Impulsive behavior**

   Acting without stopping to think or even knowing why you are behaving this way. Out-of-control behavior is not good for you or for the people around you. If you aren't careful, you will explode into anger and profanity when something comes up that you don't know how to handle.

6. Feeling overwhelmed

The world is too bright, too demanding, too fast, too much. So you tend to hide and withdraw, which only increases your feelings of helplessness. With so much going on inside of you, it is hard to do even the simplest of tasks, much less meet the demands of life in the community, develop new relationships, or look for a job.

The most effective way to deal with this upheaval is to acknowledge it as real and normal. If you try to pretend nothing is happening – *or* if you believe you will always feel this way – you will make the process harder than it has to be. I assure you the heavy changes *will* slow down and you'll have a far more secure viewpoint on everything.

Above all, don't believe in or act on the extremes of your emotions. Take it easy and give things time to settle down. If you find that your emotions or actions are dangerous to you or to others, get help immediately! And always have absolute faith that your steady efforts will pay off.

TRAPS DEALING WITH OTHER PEOPLE

7. Feelings of alienation

Viewing the whole world as "the enemy." Although you may not be consciously aware that you feel this way, it will show up in your treatment of others. And if you treat everyone as your enemy, they will respond the same way.

8. Hostile, aggressive actions

Trying to intimidate and lean on people, like others have done to you or like you did in the joint to make sure no one messed with you. Using fear to get your way doesn't work in the streets ... it just makes people cut you loose.

9. Outbursts of rage

Exploding with anger when things don't go your way – or lashing out for no apparent reason. You will be shocked the first time you catch yourself foaming at the mouth without really knowing why.

10. Resenting criticism or disapproval

Taking it as a personal insult if anyone criticizes or disagrees with your actions. You may resist any type of authority because you never again want to feel powerless as you did in prison.

11. Suspicious and unable to trust

You tend to withdraw and stand apart, not trusting the people around you ... always alert and watchful, expecting the worst.

12. Uncomfortable in society

You've brought your loneliness home with you. You feel like a ghost who doesn't really "fit" anywhere ... you just don't belong.

13. Hungry for companionship

You may feel desperate for a close personal relationship. But when you actually hook up with someone, you are far more emotionally vulnerable than you realize. This can lead you into bad choices and destructive relationships.

14. Isolated socially and emotionally

The protective walls you built around yourself in prison now stand between you and relationships in the free world. It feels as if you will suffocate, alone and cut off behind your walls.

These attitudes can hurt others, but they damage you most of all, making it harder for you to get along with loved ones, employers and co-workers, parole and law enforcement personnel, or with strangers. Carried to the extreme, some of these attitudes can lead to violent reactions that could put you back behind bars.

Keep in mind that your well-being is tied to the good graces of others, so monitor your attitude and the way you are coming across to people. If folks are stepping back from you, there is a reason – probably because you're being too heavy or intense. Recognize that your reactions are causing much of the tension, then take a deep breath and remind yourself to lighten up.

As time goes by, you will feel better among strangers. For now, spend "quality time" with a few folks you feel comfortable around. Don't rush into intimacy: look for friendship before romance, for a rewarding moment rather than a cheap thrill. Remember that good relationships are built on trust and that takes time, so you must be patient.

TRAPS DEALING WITH YOURSELF

15. False expectations of self and the world

Set you up for frustration and crushing disappointment when things don't work out the way you thought they would.

16. Desire for immediate gratification

Intense impatience to have everything "right now." When you don't get what you want right away, you may lose the motivation to keep on trying ... just give up completely.

17. Fear of failure and rejection

Often hidden behind a "bad attitude." But this creates a cycle of self-defeating thoughts and actions, because a negative, nasty attitude will drive away the very people and support you need.

18. Surrender to addictions

Helps you forget your pain and distress, but only for a little while. Over the long run, addiction is another self-defeating cycle, because it destroys your ability to cope with the demands you face.

19. Deep sense of anxiety and vulnerability

Great uncertainty about what the future holds or how to best deal with it, as if the ground might crumble out from under you at any moment.

20. Cycles of depression

Leave you feeling deeply sad, empty, lost, and dejected.

Depression is a thief that steals the energy you need to handle your situation, until you feel helpless, trapped at the bottom of a black pit. The result can be loss of hope, the greatest trap of all.

Don't let the pressure you feel in the middle of your chest endanger your re-entry into the world. The stress can be intense, so it's natural to look for ways to escape it. For many of us that means going back to things – typically drugs, alcohol, sex, or cheap thrills – that we know will make us feel better, at least take the edge off for awhile. But these "escapes" are really just another trap; they rob us of the power and focus we need to reconstruct our lives.

So stay cool and be flexible. Examine your plans and expectations regularly and make adjustments when the situation changes. Think things through and try to have a back-up plan ready when – not if – something goes wrong. It is often smart to seek guidance from people you trust who may have a clearer picture than you of what is reasonable and right to expect. Above all, keep on trying. If the next thing doesn't work, try something else. The only real failure comes when you give up.

Stop once or twice a day and look to see what's going on inside of you. Watch yourself closely ... especially any strong emotions that threaten to drag you under. Refuse to make decisions or take action while in a "dark place" – given time, it will pass! If you find yourself thinking that things can never get any better, that there's no reason to go on, reach out for help immediately. This is not a sign of reality – it is depression. Life after prison is demanding, but always remember that you have lived through far worse and come out a better person. You can endure and overcome these challenges, too.

DEALING WITH ALL OF IT

With all this going on, you can see why success after prison is so slow and demanding. It's natural to feel weighed down at times by the combined force of these issues. It is simply beyond human capacity to carry such a load and keep it under control all the time – *it cannot be done!!* So, use your experience and insight to avoid as many traps as you can. Most of the things that beat you up after prison can be resolved with fortitude, time, and patience, but some cannot. When the burden grows so great you feel things might explode, do not hesitate to reach out for help.

There are people in the community – both professional counselors and just plain folks who have learned from their own experiences – who really can help you cope with these issues. This doesn't mean they should tell you what to do or "fix" your problems for you. Their real value is helping you identify and expand your options and find solutions you didn't know existed. Always be on the lookout for such individuals – they can be a priceless treasure. Remember to treat them with the respect and appreciation they deserve ... and to pass their insight on to others when the time is right.

A word of caution: one of the hardest parts of getting help from others is simply being able to let yourself accept it. That may sound strange, but I think you know what I mean. It has always been a challenge for me to let anyone close enough to help with my most serious issues. Maybe this is out of fear they will "get off into my business" or learn how vulnerable I am. The danger is that such fears will prevent you from getting the help and support you really need. When this occurs, the past is still doing a number on you. Refuse to let your history own you: choose the future!

Don't make the mistake of thinking that you must – or even can – climb this mountain overnight or without developing new skills. This is an ongoing journey which brings increasing progress, insight, and satisfaction. Simply by choosing to face these issues, you reduce their power to control you. Many other ex-felons have overcome these obstacles – and so will you.

■ After the War Zone

"Under stress, we can turn into mad dogs, dangerous to others, but most of all to ourselves. If this keeps happening, it's time to get professional help – a little at the right time can make all the difference."

Life in prison is like living for years in a combat zone. There aren't many major battles, but there is constant danger from snipers, ambush, and booby traps. Even in your sleep, you have to be on guard for unseen dangers coming from unexpected directions. Living under this kind of stress for years on end takes a heavy toll on the survivors. The effects – some of which we have just reviewed – can last for years or a lifetime.

When we look back at wars throughout history, there is ample evidence that people have serious adjustment problems when trying to come home again. How do you live with what happened to you, as well as what you watched others go through? Inmates, like soldiers, experience many forms of emotional injury which can come back to haunt them long after release.

This is different from the tension you naturally feel in coping with survival needs; the causes for this type of "post-traumatic" stress are far deeper and don't seem to have a name or face. And because the source is so hard to identify, it seldom clears up by itself. In fact, such stress often displays itself in cycles, coming and going without any apparent cause. Some off-the-wall word or event can bring back a painful emotion or memory – a kind of flashback – that hits you right between the eyes! If this kind of stress gets you by the throat and will not let go, don't ignore it or wait for it to just go away. Instead, face the reality of your situation and seek solutions.

First, resist thinking that you must remain a victim of these "dark forces." Then seek professional help to identify and confront your ghosts. You must understand that you cannot fix some parts of yourself and ignore the others. Each element is part of a much bigger pattern: the total YOU. Although it won't happen all at once, your goal must be to improve your overall well-being, a little bit each day. The good news is that when you assist one part, all the rest benefit as well. This leads to improvements which, in turn, will encourage you to expand your efforts.

With competent help, plus great effort and courage, you can bring your distress under control and heal the damages brought on by your particular "war." Real progress is possible as long as you refuse to surrender to your demons. Above all, never give up on yourself or the value of being alive.

■ *Patience Is Essential*

"People come out of prison desperate for many things and desperate people have no patience. Have faith that if you invest enough time and effort, you will ultimately achieve the rewards you hunger for."

A big part of coping with life after prison is coming to terms with TIME. In prison, all we wanted was for time to get out of the way, to "be over." Now we are anxious and impatient because time still won't let us have everything we want instantly. This desire for instant gratification comes from desperation and the illusion that we can catch up on all we've lost during years of captivity. But time does not answer to anyone. We fight with it or flow with it ... those are our only real choices.

You can save yourself a mountain of grief by accepting reality: the first two years after a major fall will be consumed by the effort of reconstructing your life. During much of this period, your main priority is daily survival. You have to build a firm base on which your future will

stand, solid and secure. You begin with little more than a reasonable plan and a strong will, and build from there, one small step at a time. In the first few years you likely will endure a low-level job, meager pay, and sad living conditions. But don't be disheartened or crippled by emotions such as rage, fear, and self-pity. In fact, all this is normal in a strange way because it comes with being an ex-convict. It has nothing to do with your real worth as a person.

Remind yourself that your value is based on the quality of your character and behavior. As long as you keep the faith and refuse to give up, things will gradually improve and new opportunities will open themselves to you. For example, many ex-cons go through several jobs in the first year after release. As they gain experience and a work history, the jobs and the pay get better.

So have faith! Things will improve if you give them time and keep on trying. This will put you on a slow but steady path of growth toward a quality life. Above all, be ready to let your common sense guide you, not your emotions and wishful thinking. Celebrate even the smallest victory and give yourself time to achieve major progress.

Keep in mind that the first six to twelve months after release will be the most uncertain. This is generally not the time to do something big – like get married, buy a house, or open a business ... be REAL!! After you have your survival needs under control and your personal business in order, THEN you can make major life decisions, like having a baby or moving to Colorado.

Some big dreams, like owning

your own business, may be possible, but they will take even longer and you will have to pay major dues to make them happen. Expecting to make your dreams come true in the first few months or years after prison often leads to failure and despair. Instead, use your energy to build the skills, resources, and support you need to turn your ambitions into reality.

■ Special Needs of Long Termers

"After release from a long bit, you have to act on pure faith! Greet the future with an unbending belief that beauty and comfort are real and attainable. It may seem impossible, but THAT is what it takes!"

I have waited until all the other parts of this section were done before I spoke directly to persons who have done serious, long-term sentences. Be assured that everything written in this book is true and useful, no matter the length of time served. But I fully recognize and respect the fact that you will have some very special needs as you re-enter the world.

What is awaiting you out here is the same as for all ex-cons. But what is *not* out here will be distinctly different for persons who have served many years in prison. Our essential roots, the things that anchor us to life – family, social traditions, familiar buildings, types of work and technology, styles of music and fashions – many will simply have vanished. This demands that you rebuild from scratch, with the unique chance to re-define yourself and your relationship with all elements of life.

Another major difference in coming out after thirteen years, as opposed to three, is the shocking degree of change between the world you left and the one to which you return. You should expect to "come back to life" very slowly because the gap between today and the day you got flushed makes the Grand Canyon seem tiny by comparison! You have lost one of the major stages of your life – and maybe more than one. This is something you can never get back, so don't waste your time trying. Instead, focus on the present – the many rewarding moments the free world offers. Promise yourself to "keep the faith" no matter what and make the most out of what lies ahead.

Think of yourself as a grizzly bear awakening after a hard, cold winter. As you emerge from hibernation, you will feel clumsy and disoriented. At first everything will seem off balance and out of control. But this is only temporary! More than most living beings are called upon to do, you must meet your freedom with an unbending faith in yourself and in the beauty of life. The good news is that so much will be new, fresh, and glorious – just as long as you permit yourself to taste it in small bites so you won't be overwhelmed!

Let yourself live in the here and now, willing and able to feel that you actually "belong" in the free world. Your ultimate goal is to *connect* – first with small things, like privacy, the ability to come and go, and the spring breeze in your hair. Then comes a child's smile, the majesty of a mountain, the thrill of a stock car race. The possibilities are endless!

Due to the length of time you

were gone and all you went through, your renewal will take longer and be more difficult than for short-timers. But it will also be far more rewarding. Expect to build *a solid 60 months* of freedom before you feel truly connected with the world, in touch with yourself and in adequate control of your daily life. This may seem like too high a mountain to climb, but just hang in there. With each passing month, you will discover that you can stand a little straighter and breath a little deeper.

Warning: the first two or three years will contain some very low moments – isolation, emptiness, stress, and loneliness to the extreme. But they will pass! After all, life in the free world, no matter how demanding, has to be better than ending up in a prison grave yard. Your future is strongly tied to your belief that beauty, laughter, and love are real. Not only real but yours to experience! So as you can, begin to slowly take off your armor and let the sunshine in. As you do, make every effort to draw fresh energy from the wonders you discover. And above all else, *never give up!!!*

Critical Concerns

■ *The First Steps*

"You have to stay on top of your thoughts and feelings, not one day at a time, not one MINUTE at a time … but one HEART BEAT at a time!!"

As we've discussed, the first twelve months back on the streets is an *extremely* critical period. The best advice on how to handle this time is to remain calm, keep a good grip on your emotions, and focus on the things you need to do to survive. To get started, look at the action plan you developed for the first few weeks on the streets. It will give you a useful sense of direction during this very confusing time.

First, review your short-range plans. These are your immediate goals, the practical things that will begin your journey. *Be careful*: don't look at your list and let it overcome you! Remember that reconstruction is a slow process, and avoid the traps of taking on or expecting too much too soon. Work on the three to five things most essential to your needs each day. Your plan will help you set priorities and decide how to apply your limited time and resources.

At the end of each day, spend fifteen minutes evaluating your progress and making a schedule for tomorrow. When something is harder than you expected or doesn't work out as you hoped, adapt by revising your plan and readjusting your mind, energy, and resources. The keys to your success are *organization, persistence, and patience*. Your progress will come in small steps, each one building on the last. You will find that even a little progress provides a feeling of growing pride and confidence.

Before you can move forward to your long-range plans, a variety of issues must be addressed. These fall into six basic areas of concern:

1. Mental Stability
2. Legal Requirements
3. Economic Survival
4. Employment Needs

5. Social Relationships
6. Personal Development

▨ *Mental Stability*

A FOOT IN BOTH WORLDS

"Commit yourself to the higher path – to that which is hard, not easy; to what is good, not bad; to what goes forward, not backward; to what leads us beyond shame and humiliation ... onward to pride and dignity."

On the day of release, you no longer belong to the prison world, but at the same time you don't fit in the society you are re-entering. You find yourself in a No Man's Land with a foot in both worlds, inlaw and outlaw!

The resulting conflict in identities and roles, of being an "outlaw-inlaw," is a serious concern. Feeling cut off and set apart, you may decide that existing rules and responsibilities don't apply to you. In this state of mind, you flip back and forth between behavior that is legal and illegal, moral and immoral. Many ex-cons "play" legal or moral as long as things are mellow. But when threatened or overwhelmed, they shift back to the self-image of "outlaw" since it gives them a greater sense of power and control than that of "citizen."

This can result in intense danger, along with confusion and stress, yet it is a natural part of moving from prison to the free world. Stay alert: as you see it happening within you, recall that it is a stage everyone must pass through. As long as you refuse to surrender to it, it will not dominate you. Again, time and patience will help you accept that you really are free and a part of the universe. As this occurs, your identity as a positive part of the community will slowly increase.

CHEAP THRILLS

"Building a quality life after prison demands strength and discipline. This is not the time to be weak, loose, or wild!"

Many of us like the fast life; we're ready to get loose whenever the chance presents itself. Even if we've been clean and on top of our game for a long time, the temptation to get wild and crazy is like a shark, *it never sleeps!* So take heed. Whatever you are weak for – that's what will take you down quickest, be it drugs or passion or rage.

Cheap thrills gain their power through two false promises: increasing pleasure and decreasing stress. And BOTH are extremely inviting to an ex-convict! All this matters to us because it makes us vulnerable, increasing the already high risk of failure.

Rebuilding after prison demands maximum mental and emotional control – true self-discipline. You must avoid anything that puts you at risk: with the law, on the job, and in the community. Every time you are tempted to "just let yourself go," stop and consider that your hard-won stability and modest resources are precious – they must be respected and protected.

NEVER GIVE UP

"If you want to get out of a hole, use a ladder not a shovel!"

Like all ex-cons, you will have to face disappointment, along with the resulting feelings of frustration and discontent, as you work to reconstruct your life. You may even feel a sense of grief that you have lost so much of your life and so many opportunities. Such distress can, if not taken in stride, lead to loss of hope and a growing depression. In such a negative state of mind, it's easy to justify all sorts of desperate, self-destructive acts. The most common is to fall back into old ways – especially use of drugs, alcohol, and sex – to try to kill the pain!

No good … *it doesn't work!* At this point you must be tired of being under the control of the Man and random forces of the universe. The remedy is to do whatever is necessary to take control of yourself and your well-being. You can *never* justify getting weak and giving up on your efforts to create a different future for yourself. When you do slip into this, remember it is just a fleeting emotion and refuse to let it own you.

Pull yourself up and reach out for the help you need! Often the solution is to find fresh, positive energy – be it in nature, prayer, meditation, art, sports, friendships, good deeds, or powerful new ideas that help you see and feel differently. Find something that helps you bring your heart and mind to a higher level. *Do it!*

Remember this: no matter how bad things get, there is *never* justification for making them worse! Even if things get so bad you think you're going to lose your mind, never give up your hope, dignity, or pride. Although jails and prisons are small and limited, the free world is huge and full of opportunity. If you're determined enough, you *can and will* find what you need to survive and feel good about yourself.

THERE'S NO GOING BACK

"Catching up is impossible. The past is dead … all we have is NOW, this moment. So live in the present and savor every breath of free air."

Many ex-prisoners try to play "catch up," to make up for all the years they wasted in prison instead of creating a career or family life – something they can be proud of. Such an attitude may be completely understandable, but *it just doesn't work*. You cannot turn back the clock. *What's done is done. What's gone is gone.*

You can't cram seven lost years into seven months; you just end up driving yourself crazy and accomplishing nothing. Instead, start where you are now and build from there. You may feel that you've missed out on an entire period of your life, but it's impossible to go back and relive it now. If you try to reach for too much, too fast, it will endanger the things you *can* realistically achieve.

Don't dwell on the things you've missed. Instead, dedicate yourself to making the rest of your life as fulfilling as possible. Remember, the world continues to turn and you are now part of that change! So go with it, flow with it. Enjoy each new day and be glad that you have a fresh chance to feel good about yourself and everything around you.

EXPECT REJECTION

"Rejection hurts but it's not the end of the world. Acknowledge your sorrow and anger, then move on ... you have far more important things to deal with!"

It's absurd to expect the world to welcome you with open arms even though you feel that you've "paid your debt to society." Get clear on this: *it isn't over!* The fact you've been released doesn't mean people are ready to accept you. Knowing you will face rejection doesn't make it easy to handle ... in fact, it can upset you to the extreme! But as an ex-con you must expect mistrust and not let it overwhelm you.

On the other hand, don't get defensive and go looking for rejection around every corner – thinking that every time things don't go your way, it's because you just walked out of a cell. This kind of attitude can keep you from making friends and harm your relationships with those who love and respect you.

Face it, people reject each other every day and it has nothing to do with a criminal background. It's a part of daily life; don't let it eat you up. Just because some people expect the worst, *don't give them what they want.* This doesn't mean you have to enjoy being treated like a leper, but don't be shocked when it happens. Of course it will bother you, *but refuse to let it break your heart!* You have far more important things to worry about, so shrug it off and move on.

GET OUT OF MY FACE!

"Never let anything or anyone drive you over the edge ... constantly remind yourself that your freedom and all it offers you is the top priority."

Most prisoners have an intense dislike of authority that spills over to life after release. After being under someone's control for so long, they are super-sensitive to the slightest hint that someone is trying to control their lives. Many go to extremes, venting their rage and aggression on anyone who doesn't give them what they want when they want it or who even appears to criticize them.

If you aren't real careful, you will take out your hostility against your loved ones, parole officer, employer, co-workers, or just a citizen who makes the mistake of getting in your face. Obviously this is dangerous! If you turn your anger and resentment against someone because they have some form of power or authority, it can cost you everything and leave you with nothing.

When we look back on such events, we always ask ourselves, "How could I be that stupid!?" Actually it is remarkably easy ... we just have to let years of shame, grief, and pain take over for one split second as we explode like a volcano! The result of such explosions is too often the kiss of death to our hope of a positive future!

Avoid this serious trap by working to keep your stress under control and reminding yourself that *freedom is the top priority*. Refuse to be a slave of your emotions. Don't let anything or anyone drive you over the edge. Be like a fish that calmly watches the bait float by *and refuses to strike*. Not because he isn't hungry, but because he is smarter than he is hungry!

You cannot control what others do to you, but you CAN control how you react!! The last thing you want is to go off into a blind rage and do damage to yourself or to another. If the weight of your emotional burden gets so extreme that you might, in fact, become violent, do the right thing ... seek professional help immediately. Find a way to control yourself or someone else will do it for you!

◼ *Legal Requirements*

UNDER SUPERVISION

"If your lifestyle makes you a target for revocation, CHANGE IT!"

The system wants to keep you on a leash as long as possible. As a result, many prisoners are placed under some form of supervision in the community, usually parole or Federal probation. In this case, like it or not, *you are still doing time*. Most important, you must cope with a set of restrictive rules that can be a slippery slope back to prison. If you violate them, you can be revoked – which you obviously want to avoid!

Above all, you have to adapt to the fact that someone will be watching you, showing up at your house, asking you questions, requiring you to report and take drug tests – holding you accountable for what you do and how you do it. Now, if all this actually worked the way it's supposed to, it would be bad but tolerable. For many prisoners, however, supervision seems like an endless series of unjustified hassles and stress. This is the nature of bureaucracy: lots of rules and not much flexibility.

With all the demands you face after release, it is easy to miss, ignore, bend, or break your supervision requirements, which often seem in conflict with your efforts to rebuild your life. Beware: half of the people arriving in prison each year are there because their parole or probation has been revoked. So it is essential that you learn and follow the rules of supervision in the streets – no matter how inconvenient or unfair they seem. Breaking a rule is considered a "technical violation" of your parole or probation, and that can flush you just as easily as a fresh conviction. You may slide on minor infractions, but if you get off into a serious trap, your slack behavior will come back to haunt you. Above all, be especially careful to report when required and keep your supervisor informed of your current address and job changes.

No one ever likes the nit-picking nature of parole or mandatory supervision but always remember – it is an improvement over daily life on a loud, nasty cell block. Be careful – the longer you're out, the more you tend to forget just how bad it was. As this occurs, your resentment at being under someone's thumb can increase until it puts you in danger of getting sideways with the system and having your parole revoked. So stay alert and remember to keep yourself humble ... or the Man will drop a bomb on you. This means keeping your act tight and not doing anything stupid. Never let your guard down – never get loose, never assume that you can joke or say anything you haven't thought through carefully. I can assure you that being on parole is much like riding a modified Harley-Davidson: the very moment you think you're in control, *it kills you!*

Caution: persons on probation and parole sometimes find they can't pay supervision and treatment fees, fines, restitution, etc., due to lack of income. You can get so stressed and uptight over this that you don't report as required. Do yourself a big favor: no matter how much pressure you're under, don't get so fearful that you fail to report. And never use the situation as an excuse to pick up a pistol or make a "big score." You *might* be revoked for failing to pay fees or coming up with a dirty drug test (usually not), but you are more likely to be revoked for failure to report or if you pick up a new charge.

One of your great challenges is to "avoid the appearance of impropriety." This means that, in addition to staying crime-free, you also must avoid anything that makes it *look like* you are up to something. For example, gang activity or hanging with known felons. In addition, some crimes create far more heat than others. If you were convicted of an extremely violent or sex-related act, you're so "visible" you probably glow in the dark! So armed robbers have to be more careful about what they do than people who went down for car theft.

Thus there are different degrees of scrutiny you may have to live under, running from quite modest to super extreme. But no matter what level of control you are under, it is always a serious situation that can threaten your new freedom. So stay alert and avoid anything or anybody that makes you a target!

RELATIONSHIP WITH YOUR P.O.

"Be honest when asked a direct question, don't volunteer any information, and prepare yourself in advance to be as cool as a clam!"

While under supervision, a third of your welfare is generally based on following the rules and not breaking any new laws. The other two-thirds depends on your interaction with your parole or probation officer. Since the relationship you develop with your P.O. is critical to your future, it is in your best interest to keep a good attitude toward such folks.

Remember: just as you want the Man to treat *you* like an individual worthy of dignity and respect, this is a *two-way street*. Don't approach your parole officer as an enemy who represents nothing but problems. Instead, be positive. Treat him or her as an individual, someone who may have both good and bad traits and with whom you wish to maintain a positive relationship. This usually works, especially if you give it enough time.

The best you can hope for from a P.O. is "reasonable fairness." You can live with that! In the beginning, it is typical for a P.O. to be hard-nosed and flex his or her authority. This is also a way of testing you, putting you under pressure to see how you react. Keep your emotions in tight control and don't show resentment or rebellion in your eyes, words, or actions. In a few months the edge will (usually) come off, once a basic level of trust develops.

Unfortunately, there is rapid turnover in supervision personnel, and just when you finally have a good understanding with one, he or she will suddenly vanish and the whole trip begins again. This can be nerve-racking, but you have to stay calm and collected. It's part of the experience of being under supervision, so you just have to deal with it.

In reality, most people get flushed for displaying a pattern of lies and screw ups over time, not just one single, isolated event. In most cases, parole and probation officers are so covered up with work that they don't have time to jack with you *unless* they view you as a "problem." This usually means: 1) you have a terrible rap sheet and they feel it wise to keep you on a short leash; 2) you are ripping and running, representing a high risk to the community; or 3) you are a constant screw up or have a bad attitude that makes you more trouble than you're worth.

Obviously, you will have a much easier time dealing with your P.O. if you don't fall into any of these categories. It's too late to change the first, but it's up to you avoid the second and third. A positive relationship with your P.O. can be really helpful if you ever run into trouble, for instance, if you're having a hard time paying your fees or get picked up as a "suspicious character." And being realistic, at some point everybody gets off into a jam without meaning to do anything wrong ... a result of being in the wrong place at the wrong time. In situations like this, if you have been generally solid in other ways, that puts you ahead

of 70% of their case load and worthy of some reasonable consideration.

Most problems, with time and patience, can be resolved. But sometimes human personalities just clash and nothing can be done to change it. If this happens and you've done everything in your power to get along, you can request a transfer to another P.O. But no matter what you do, *always report. And keep your emotions and reactions under control in all situations.*

PRE-RELEASE CENTERS AND HALFWAY HOUSES

"It's dangerous to think you are free when, in fact, you've simply transferred to another form of captivity – a prison without bars."

Many prisoners will be transferred to a pre-release or work release center before their release date or assigned to a halfway house after release. If this happens, take the following suggestions very seriously.

Be super careful while you are living in any type of transition center. Although it is a step up from a prison, *you are not free.* Such places can be deadly traps if you go in with the illusion that you are now at liberty. After years in the truly heavy atmosphere of a prison, the nature of a transition or treatment facility can seem Mickey Mouse. But if you let yourself get sideways with the situation, even for ten minutes, you are subject to find yourself back in the joint before you even know you've left!

No matter what, always remember that they are extensions of the penitentiary, not extensions of the community. They are located in the free world, but that doesn't mean they offer you the freedom of choice and action you hunger for. Prisoners who exit to a halfway house, pre-release center, or treatment program of any kind should think of it as the last part of their sentence, not the first part of their release.

Despite this, a transition facility can be useful in your efforts to reconstruct your life. Each one will be different in terms of how it operates and what it can do for you. So you need to walk in with a good attitude and find out what kind of help it offers and what you have to do to fit in. Don't count on getting all the help you need, but be ready to take advantage of whatever is there. And remember – stay alert, watch your stress levels, keep your mouth shut, follow the rules ... *and be careful!*

YOUR CRIMINAL HISTORY

"To hide from our past is impossible ... the computer never forgets. Instead, we must live each day to the best of our ability, applying ourselves to positive growth and achievement."

Time to be painfully direct: your prison term was not the end of your criminal justice involvement. To quote the warning sign to shoplifters at your local Wal-Mart store, your criminal record "will haunt you for the rest of your life."

Even if you do not have a term of post-release supervision, you face lifelong consequences related to your criminal record. Your criminal history gives you a higher risk of being re-arrested, convicted, and getting a more severe sentence. Other consequences may include the loss

of physical freedoms (such as the right to travel to other states or countries), loss of civil rights (such as the right to vote or serve on juries), and limits on many opportunities for employment or advancement. Although some of these consequences may go away after a time, others will always be with you, popping up when you least expect them. For example, years after release you could still be turned down for a home mortgage, car loan, insurance, or lease on an apartment.

In short, the day you caught a felony conviction, you came under the tireless eye of the government and the world. Anyone who wants to check you out can do so. Today most felons are listed on a computer network that can report on your background in a matter of minutes. This fact, which would have been considered fantasy only 20 years ago, is rapidly eliminating all hope of escape from your past. Some people go through the legal system to seek a pardon or have their records expunged, but these are costly and time-consuming processes that aren't practical or possible for most ex-prisoners. And in most cases, your criminal history can still be brought up in the sentencing phase of a future conviction.

This means that, in some ways, you are a criminal-for-life. If you stole a car at 20, you will still be living under the shadow of that action when you turn 70. Long after your release, you will still be accountable for your past in some way, still under some type of microscope. So, how do you best handle this? If there is no way to truly "get over" a criminal record, you have no choice but to learn to *manage* it as effectively as possible.

Before all else, make yourself a smaller target by living a moderate lifestyle and keeping a low profile. The most obvious way to do this is not to commit any crimes. And stay away from places where outlaw activity is coming down or might be expected. Use your common sense – don't drive through the dope house district at 2 a.m., even if you are just on your way home from visiting your sister. Do all you can to reduce the risk that you will get caught up in some trap, like a raid or random traffic stop. For example, pulling out of a bar at closing time makes you a prime candidate for a DUI, not to mention resisting arrest. I mean, come on, the police are sitting across the street waiting for you!

Next, be careful who you hang with. People are more likely to get in trouble with a running buddy than when alone ... plus that's who usually flips on you! You can't afford to inherit anyone's heat or be sucked into their action. Think first, and don't do something you'll regret that puts you back in a cell for another Christmas eve. You've got to use good judgment!!

In practical terms, it is possible you could be arrested at any time, whether you're doing something illegal or not. But don't be paranoid and see danger behind every corner, just be reasonable and keep your business right and tight. For the first few years after release you are in a weak position because you don't have a lot of money, friends, or resources. Plus, behavior that seems perfectly cool to you may not be tolerated in the neighborhood where you live. All this places you at higher risk of getting in trouble than the average citizen.

If you are stopped or arrested for any reason, you will need maximum self control – *especially of your mouth!* Force yourself to be polite and, if necessary, go peacefully. Many ex-cons experience painful flashbacks or even feel sick to their stomachs when handcuffed and thrown into the back of a squad car. Even when the bottom falls out, don't lose heart because, in most cases, an arrest does not send you back to the pen. The main rule here is never make a bad situation worse.

If you have so much heat on you that you are constantly being jacked with, it's smart to consult a reputable criminal lawyer. You can consider the fee a form of "legal insurance" in case you are busted. Just knowing that you have some backup can help you manage the shock, fear, and uncertainty of such a moment.

The best way to manage your criminal history is to mentally define yourself as the person you are striving to become – not an ex-con, but a person of quality and worth. Then live up to that vision of yourself. Refuse to be a captive of the past. You can't make your past disappear or avoid the consequences of your criminal record, but you don't have to let that control your mind or limit your self-worth. While it is true you have a criminal history, you also possess the ability to transform yourself and your place in the world from a negative to a positive. Although the record never goes away, many of us have been successful at this transition, and you can be as well.

▪ *Economic Survival*

NO EASY MONEY!

"Money is not a god to be worshipped nor a magical remedy for our problems. It is just one of the tools we need to reach our goals."

On the TV game show *Wheel of Fortune,* people spin the wheel and shout, "Come on easy money!!" The same thing is also said in countless crap games as people hope the next roll of the dice will send them home with a pocket full of cash. One problem ... "easy money" is a fantasy! Check it out: Las Vegas was built on the fortune suckers *left* there, not on what they took home!!

Money is a strange issue; we live in a society that seems to worship it. Too many people define success as having enough wealth and toys. We often use money to measure our self-worth and place in the world. It's as if we believe that money can solve all problems and take all pain away ... but it cannot! Don't get me wrong, money is essential to survive in our society, but thinking it is all-powerful is a dangerous illusion. Money by itself can never make life meaningful.

However, for former prisoners, money looks like the key to fulfilling our dreams of rapid reconstruction. So we want it and want it right now. And we may resent the fact that others have resources and opportunities we think should be ours. Why should we be poor or in need when other people have money to burn? Being down and out may seem like a good excuse for taking what isn't ours, but this is totally false! If our impatience or envy tells us it's OK to take what other people have, we're headed back to prison!

Remember: your worth as a person can't be measured by how much money you have, nor by comparing your possessions with someone else's. You must build your future on what you can bring in *without doing harm* to yourself or to others. You do this by turning your effort and time into useful labor which you exchange for cash – that is, *you earn it.* Why? Because in reality, "there ain't no free lunch." Plus, what you gain from personal achievement pays triple in pride and satisfaction ... something we all desire.

BEWARE OF DESPERATION

"Eating rocks for breakfast is a stage we all go through the first couple of years after release. Don't get so discouraged that you believe it will always be like this. Have faith in a better day and just keep cooking."

Most ex-prisoners hit the bricks with little or nothing to stand on. In this situation, it doesn't seem that you have many choices – you are ready to do whatever it takes to get by. The obvious danger is that, while trying to survive, you may do something that places you at risk of re-arrest. No good!! Even though you will be stretched to the limit of your modest resources, you cannot permit anything to put you back in a cell. Gradually, with effort, time, and six carloads of determination, you will achieve the security you seek. No one who has done this will say it is easy or quick ... but it is definitely worth it!

While money cannot buy happiness, you are nevertheless in serious trouble if you don't have any. And that is never more true than when they kick you out of the pen with no place to go and no way to get there. Things can get really tough when your money runs out (assuming you had any to start with) and you have nothing to eat, no job, no transportation ... zero.

Poverty brings with it a special distress, a form of depression combined with intense desperation. And desperate people can justify just about anything in order to survive. But I warn you not to let poverty drive you to steal or stick a .45 up someone's nose. That is wrong – for many reasons – and in the end it will harm you as much as your victim. If you jump back into illegal activity, no matter what the reason, the law of averages has you targeted for another fall, or worse. Better to be skinny in the streets than fat in the joint. Earning the minimum wage in the free world *has* to be better than 17 cents an hour in some prison industry.

As in all times of high stress, it is essential to keep yourself under control. Don't try to escape from the weight of the moment by drinking or drugging; it just makes things worse. This is why it's so important to develop a survival plan *before* you get out. When caught up in desperate moments, go back and look at what you planned when your mind was clearer. Remember that there are ways to survive without hurting people or breaking the law, so find and follow them.

Be prepared to ask for help if that's what it takes. Often you have to turn to people who care about you; in such cases you must be care-ful not to abuse their generosity. Also, most communities have social service agencies or faith-based groups that can provide some kinds of assistance, but you have to seek it out. Don't let pride get in the way: when you get back on your feet, you will have the chance to pass on the favor by helping someone else.

BUILD A NEST EGG

"When you have an extra buck, don't spend it. STASH IT!"

Considering how hard you have to work for your money, take care to hang on to it whenever you can. Continue to develop a budget for your future needs just as you did for your survival. If you keep track of where your money is going, you may be able to find ways to cut your spending in order to increase your savings and security. Use your budget as a tool to help you achieve your long-range goals.

In the beginning you will be hurting for cash and have to spend what little you have on basic survival. But once you are able to handle your essential needs, the time will come when you have an extra buck in your pocket. When you do, don't spend it; *stash it!* Build a nest egg, just a tiny bit at a time. Put it in a savings account where you won't be tempted to blow it on one wild weekend. I assure you that just having a few hundred dollars set aside will greatly improve your sense of security. This lean period right after release is NOT permanent. Consider everything you do and every penny you save as an investment in a more positive future.

◼ *Employment Needs*

FINDING A JOB

"Employers need workers they can count on. If you show them you really want to work and give them some basis for trusting you, you WILL find a job!"

While it's important that you relax and enjoy your return to freedom, it is equally important that you begin putting your life back on track as soon as possible. And one of the most basic steps in this process is to find employment. You can expect to experience a *lot* of resistance and frustration as you look for a job. OPEN's book *Man, I Need a Job!* (see the back of this book for information) covers much of what you need to know in order to be successful; I advise you to read it *immediately.* It also has information to help your family understand your situation and how they can help.

As you pursue a job, keep the following in mind. First, you are broke and under great pressure to survive. Second, you have the system (and even your family) telling you to find a job and pay fees, fines, and living expenses. Third, you are anxious to reconstruct your life. And, fourth, you want to rebuild your self-worth by becoming financially self-reliant. That's a lot to carry!!

With so much pressure on you, you need a job and you need it NOW. All this stress can become too much for any one person to handle, especially if you don't get hired right away. Plus, after a dozen rejections, it's easy to fall into a deep depression and adopt a negative attitude. To keep this from happening, you must constantly review the following facts:

1. Job hunting is never, ever easy for anyone, so you have to stick with it and have faith that the law of averages will take care of you.

2. Finding a job is a special skill in itself; the more you practice, the better you get.

3. Do not link your self-worth with acceptance or rejection by an employer or fellow employee. Remember that your worth as a person is determined by what you do, not by other people's reactions to you.

4. You can always improve your situation by developing new skills – so stay on the lookout for ways to get more education and training. Go get them! Keep growing!!

5. Every attempt moves you closer to success. Once you have a job, no matter what it is, it is much easier to find a better one.

As with any major effort, preparation is *critical!!!* Start with an honest review of your strengths and weaknesses as an employee. Then develop a job search plan to take advantage of your strong points and compensate as much as you can for the weak ones. This will help you organize your time and focus on efforts that have the best chance of success. Once you have a solid plan, keep at it; don't give up. Being consistent and persistent are major keys to success in job hunting.

Former prisoners often believe the world is against them because of their criminal past. This can be a huge trap, because anger and resentment begin to cloud your vision, and your attitude can become hostile and hopeless. Then you are tempted to lose the faith and motivation you need to continue the fight. If this happens and you don't understand that *finding a job is a job in itself*, it can simply break your heart!! No matter how difficult, no matter how many attempts don't work out, refuse to let it rob you of hope. Just stick with it and you will score.

The good news is that employers are always looking for people who are motivated, trustworthy, and ready to put in a good day's work. If you walk in with a positive attitude, *you will find a job!*

YOUR CRIMINAL RECORD

"It's usually better to take the heat up front and then prove yourself, rather than sneak in the back door and constantly fear the day they find out the truth and slam dunk you."

For the rest of your life you will be faced with questions regarding your criminal history, especially when you apply for a job. Because it has such an important role in your future, it is essential to prepare for this issue both before and after release. OPEN's book ***Man, I Need a Job!*** (see the back of this book for information) has a special section on how to handle this matter in a constructive way.

Your criminal history will seriously impair your ability to earn a living, especially for the first three to five years after release. So you will have to be painfully realistic. The jobs that are easier for you to get may not appeal to you and they sure won't make you rich, but they will cover your living expenses until you can find something better. And like many other people, you may also have to work a second job to get enough to live on.

Also realize that some jobs may be closed to you or harder to get because of your criminal record or the nature of your offense. Be sure to research any legal or policy restrictions before you start your job search or get specialized training. Don't ignore this reality: it may come back to haunt you just when you're counting on a particular opportunity to rebuild your life. As painful as it may be, it is far better to know in advance!

KEEPING A JOB

"If your performance is great but your attitude SUCKS, you can count on finding yourself outside the door looking in!"

Once you have a job, you need to hold on to it until you find a better opportunity. And whenever you do leave, you need it to be by your choice, not by necessity.

Many ex-inmates lose jobs for some very simple mistakes. If an employer is paying for your work, he expects you to be *on time* and to be there every day. As a new employee, you can't expect to have much sick leave to use up, so don't waste it on a Monday-morning hangover. And when you're on the job, be alert and ready for *whatever* needs doing. If someone is willing to pay you to do it, the job is important enough for you to do well.

A key requirement for keeping a job is getting along with others. You'd be shocked how many people are run off because they get into a beef with a co-worker or threaten a foreman's life. It doesn't matter who is in the right, because no employer can endure having people at each other's throat. And if somebody has to go, it's usually the ex-con ... *so do your best to find positive ways to resolve differences!*

Another big problem for many ex-cons is that they are not willing to accept supervision. They may feel smarter than their boss or other employees and think they could do a better job. Or they may not be comfortable admitting it when they make mistakes or don't know what to do. But neither attitude is reasonable. What they are really saying is: I'm out of the joint now, and nobody can tell me what to do! This is very dangerous because no one will tolerate a hostile know-it-all who refuses to take orders.

So be careful – watch the way you react!! Be ready to accept instruction and criticism with a positive attitude, as a way for you to grow and improve. The faster you learn the requirements of your job, the more effective you can be as an employee and the sooner you will be granted more recognition, responsibility, and higher pay. As you strive to build a place for yourself in a new job and new life, humility is a very smart approach.

BE YOUR OWN BOSS?

"Self-employment is a long-range goal that requires serious preparation. Jumping into it before you're ready is like trying to swim the Atlantic Ocean ... be smart and build a good boat!"

For many newly released inmates, self-employment is a long-held dream. It seems to offer the advantages of a job, without the drawbacks that many former felons dread. After being bossed around and treated like an idiot for years, you want to run your own show and give the orders instead of taking them. Also, it seems like a reasonable way to avoid disclosing your criminal history and facing the possibility of rejection.

Think again. Self-employment is typically out of the reach of most ex-cons until they have spent three to five years building a solid base in the community. Running your own business is probably the *hardest* way to get started after release, not the easiest. You will have to work longer and harder for yourself than for an employer and at far greater risk. Plus, you will need money to cover start-up costs and monthly expenses until some cash starts coming in. Despite the rumors floating around prisons, there are no easy loans, disability payments, or free tools and trucks waiting for you when you get out. And don't think that working for yourself will eliminate the risk of rejection. It's just that the rejection will come from creditors and potential customers rather than from potential employers.

Don't get me wrong – working for yourself can be very rewarding, both personally and financially. But success will not come easy or quick. It will take planning and persistence. Spend your first three years in the community building the resources you will need – skills, money, tools, relationships. Get up-to-date on new techniques and ways of doing business. Ask for advice. Develop a business plan and ask knowledgeable people to review it. That way you can plug the holes so you don't set sail in a sinking ship. In other words, if being self-employed is your dream, be prepared to pay the price to put the odds for success on your side.

■ Social Relationships

YOU AND THE COMMUNITY

"No matter what has happened in your life, always treat other people the way you want them to treat you. That does more to gain their cooperation and respect than anything else in the world."

Most of us fall out of the joint with a set of "attitudes" about ourselves and others – and much of this is cold, negative, and hostile. We maintain this "armor" as a way of saying, "Don't jack with me!" And while this may have worked well in prison, it will not get us where we want to go in the free world. But these "bad attitudes" took time to develop and cannot be changed overnight or just because we want to. Over the first few years it's as if a black cloud follows us wherever we go, often casting a shadow over what we think, say, and do. And, from time to time, when we least expect it, a bolt of lightning will blast out and strike us and everyone around us.

Much of our hostility comes from

being powerless and out of touch for so long, plus not knowing how to handle being pulled in so many directions at once. When the stress gets too great, we need to release some of our deepest pain and resentment. Such a "release" needs to be positive and constructive, without giving way to anger and rage. If we strike out blindly, with no control, we end up doing great damage to everyone involved, including ourselves.

You can do a lot to reduce the chance of such disasters by knowing what to look out for and catching yourself before you get carried away. The more aware you are of these dangers, the greater your ability to handle them effectively, so let's stop and look at a few.

1. Refuse to fall off into fits of blind rage or self-pity. Declaring war on the world for all the bad things which have come down on you and your people is an exercise in futility. You will know it is happening when you see yourself displaying a nasty, poisonous manner to friends and strangers alike. They don't deserve it and simply will not put up with it!! People will strongly resist or simply get the hell away from you – leaving you even more isolated and alone. Remember that you are now free to alter your life, to move away from past grief and toward achievement. Refuse to be a puppet of your past. Get up and move on!

2. Equally destructive is any effort to "catch back" on those who have betrayed or abandoned you. It can only end in ruin – I know.

Causing pain for others will not wipe out your anger and suffering. Instead it can and will destroy your chance of creating the future you desire.

3. Prison was a tiny, ugly world – why bring it home with you? Now that you are out, don't waste your time recalling the pain and loneliness. Make a conscious effort to quit reliving the suffering you and your loved ones have endured. And resist the temptation to play the old game of "scaring the squares" with some "Billy bad ass" attitude and prison war stories. Yes, some of this is unavoidable, but don't make it harder for a citizen to accept you by trying to be cold or tough. If you're not careful, you'll constantly talk about life in prison and how heavy your experiences were! This is normal since it's all you have to refer to, but it turns people off and you don't get what you want or need. Instead of dwelling on the past, make every effort to be positive and look ahead to new things.

4. Prison life was built on control of one person or group by another. All ex-cons, at some point, catch themselves trying to control things around them just as they were controlled. But this attitude will only cause more resentment and imbalance of power, and that is what you want to leave behind. If you catch yourself doing this, stop and realize that you don't have to put other people down before you can get up yourself. And it doesn't make you any less of a person if other people don't always see things

your way. Remember, your own personal dignity and sense of self-worth are the result of how you feel about yourself and the way you live your life.

5. All this can lead to a general crusade of hate and vengeance which can only result in your destruction. If you decide that everyone is the enemy, then you will wage war on anyone you come in contact with. But there are millions of folks in the world. You can never win against them all, so why start something that must eventually lead to your own ruin? Remember: the goal is to get up and get over, not to be snuffed or stranded in a homeless shelter, mental hospital, or ad seg unit!!

Until you can overcome, or at least control, your anger and fear of rejection, you will end up driving away the very people you need to like and support you. This is self-defeating and can only increase your misery. The best way to relate to citizens is to focus on what matters to them. Look around and make mental note of new issues and current events. Direct your discussions toward *positive* things happening in daily living and the concerns you have in common with others. This takes a conscious effort the first six months after release, but with practice you will greatly improve your ability to relate to people and feel much more comfortable doing it.

Last, keep this in mind: when hitting the streets, you *immediately* come face to face with attitudes and actions totally opposite from those you've been dealing with every day.

This includes the rules people interact by, the meaning of words and body language. *Just* like the shock of going down and the series of earthquakes that followed, you face the same upheavals when you return. But it's OK; you just have to learn the current rules of the game. You have what it takes to do this, let there be no doubt.

Fortunately, in the free world you can become known more for *what you do* than where you've been! So if you prove over a period of time that you are a real and decent person, *that* is how others will view you. The secret to this is really no secret at all: *be honest and practice the Golden Rule.* This means treating others as you want to be treated. Nothing else works!!! No matter what has happened in your life, by treating others the way you want them to treat you, you do more to gain their cooperation and respect than anything else in the world. Equally important, you will have more and more respect for yourself. And I give you my word that self-respect is a treasure worth working for.

MANY WELLS BUT NO BUCKET ...

"No one is standing around waiting to help an ex-convict. You have to earn the cooperation of those who control the resources you need."

Tons of false information gets passed around behind bars about all the wonderful programs and opportunities awaiting newly released prisoners. This is, for the most part, wishful thinking and *absolute garbage*.

The attitude of many citizens and politicians is that helping ex-cons is like doing them a favor ... as if they are rewarding someone for committing a crime. From this point of view, to help you put your life in order isn't reasonable and doesn't make good sense. You may ask, *"How do they expect me to do right if I don't have any help?"* But, to be totally honest, most citizens are too busy with the details of their daily lives to consider what is happening to ex-prisoners or their families. This attitude, valid or not, is common in the world you are re-entering, for better or worse! This is the way it is, so don't waste your time sniveling about it. Instead, learn how to deal with it and refuse to let anything overcome you.

It simply doesn't pay to come out into the world expecting help based on your criminal history. If you ask for help because you are a habitual felon with good intentions, usually all you get is a boot in the rear! There are exceptions, but it takes years to find them and that isn't useful right after release. Instead, you have to find a better, more effective way to sell yourself, ensure your survival, and obtain the support needed to put your life together. Be assured that it can be done; you just have to be upbeat and persistent.

A PERSON IN NEED

"Who are you?? A highly motivated person seeking an opportunity to survive and to prosper."

To be successful in your approach to the free world, you have to understand how the community works. If society thinks it's wrong to help an ex-con, then *re-define who you are* so that you have a better shot at community acceptance. It may sound silly, but you'd be amazed how successful you will be if you open your mind and use this reconstruction period as a unique opportunity to "re-define yourself."

So if you're not a criminal just out of prison, then who are you?? A lot of different things, but before all else, *you're a human being,* then you are a man or woman, then a citizen, then a parent, then a job seeker, then way down the list, you're an "ex-convict." The problem is that in your mind the day of exit, the ex-con label is at the top of your list ... a perfect example of how reality can get turned upside down.

When dealing with the community, before all else you have to modify the way you see yourself, shifting from outsider to insider. Until you do this, you will have a real problem in representing yourself effectively. *First,* you are a "person" – capable, motivated, determined, sincere, and willing to treat others with dignity and respect! *Next,* you are a citizen who cares about the community and the welfare of others. *Third,* you are a hard worker, sincere in your desire to be trustworthy and render a good day's work. *THIS is who you are!*

You see, community service agencies exist to serve not *"ex-cons"* but *"people in need."* However, no one agency or program can serve everyone so each has a special focus as to what they do and who they serve. Any given community resource is not "good" or "bad," just different in what it does and how.

The secret to success in most cases is properly *matching* your needs with a community resource that serves those needs. Your job is to offer them a well-intended *person* who needs their services and *closely fits* their guidelines. That is, you want to be identified as eligible for their services. You need to help them see you as an *ideal client* ... no hassles, no sweat. This means re-defining your needs and qualifications to best fit the services they offer.

Obviously you cannot obtain something if it doesn't exist in your community! But, if it *does,* you can often figure out a way to qualify, because you are in fact "a human being in need of resources and support!" On this level, *you are as much entitled to help as anyone else.* Common sense is essential, of course: a man does not quality for pre-natal care. And it's never good to give false information; it catches up with you and poisons your future efforts. But when you have a reasonable chance to qualify for a service, be creative and don't give up.

When asking an agency for help, always remember that they don't owe you anything. While they may exist to help others, they generally refuse to put up with any bull! So be polite and keep yourself under control, no matter how much stress you are under or how much jive they put you through. If you absolutely hit the wall with someone who refuses to grant you assistance you are eligible for, ask to speak with a supervisor rather than go to war.

In the beginning just collect information. Find out everything you can about what they offer and exactly who they help; then "re-design yourself" to fit. Do it by phone, mail, or the Internet (if you don't have a computer, go to the local library). This is an acquired skill that builds with practice. You can get real good at it by the fourth time you go through it. Eventually *it does pay off;* it's how I was able to find the support needed to attend college. All this takes work, but when you're on the bottom trying to get up, it's worth it!!

■ *Personal Development*

IN PURSUIT OF YOUR GOALS

"Positive growth comes in countless shapes and sizes, all valuable because they move you forward toward a richer, more fulfilling life."

What matters in the streets is what mattered to us as prisoners: our freedom, our family, our future. But our focus is different when we think about these concerns in the community as opposed to a cell block. Our goal following release is not just to get out but to stay out. Not only to keep our families from deserting us but to create a rewarding relationship that benefits both them and us. Not only to exist but to thrive as we move forward into the remainder of our lives. These are our goals now, as free members of society.

And the best way to achieve these goals is to remain arrest-free for five full years. Why? Because if you can stay out of the system for 60 months, you have learned what it takes to stay out forever. So, as we discussed in part one of this book, establish this as your central goal, constantly seeking ways to increase your odds of success. And when you reach your fifth year of freedom, *celebrate!!*

Whenever you find it hard to stay motivated and focused, remind yourself of what truly matters. While the system may think that ex-cons are best controlled by the threat of "being sent back," our true motivation comes from the chance to achieve a more rewarding future.

Thus, when things get outrageous, stop and consider the supreme importance of personal freedom, of being with people you value, and having the chance to actively pursue your hopes and dreams. Then get yourself back on track and move forward.

STAY REAL!

"Every dream composed in the darkness of a cell must be tested in the light of day following release – not only can it be done, but when, where, and how."

Remind yourself that a lot of the "plans" you made while laid up in a cage were really "wishes" you needed to keep hope alive. That is what all prisoners do – it's a natural response to an unnatural situation. So after release, you must be super careful to test your dreams to make sure they have a basis in practical reality. This includes an honest review of the skill, resources, time, support, and commitment it will take to transform hope into reality.

This doesn't mean you should give up on your dreams, rather you should strive to get your head, heart, and hustle all moving in the same practical direction! An ex-con simply cannot afford to become distracted by or invested in illusion, no matter how appealing it may be. This is true on ALL levels – people, situations, opportunities, and the speed of change. You have to deal with reality as it is, not as you wish it to be!

When you have a hard time telling the difference between jail house wishes and real world facts, seek out someone of good heart and sound judgment who knows how the world actually works. Discuss the plans you made in prison to see if and how they will work out here in the free world. Set your ego aside and open your mind. What you discover may disappoint you, but it will keep you from setting yourself up to fail!! Use this person's insight and experience to give your plans a reality based tune-up. Do not throw your hands up and walk away just because things aren't as you expected. Instead, be encouraged that you now have goals that can actually be achieved!

When you decide to seek this level of support, a few firm rules apply.

- Be painfully honest; don't bend the truth or play any games.
- Show real respect and never violate the trust that is granted you.
- Remember to say "thank you" ... and mean it!
- And accept the duty of passing on to others the love and kindness that has been shown to you.

EDUCATION AND TRAINING

"The best way to get up the quickest is to go back to school!"

For an ex-con, the best and most practical way to achieve your dreams of a quality future is to expand your mind and skills. Therefore, as soon as you possibly can, *go learn something positive!* This has two major advantages: first, it is great for your motivation, bringing fresh energy, hope, and achievement. Second,

your ability to get along in the world, to be productive and improve the quality of your life, always increases as your mind and abilities expand. There is no down side ... self-improvement is always a winner!

So once you have time and attention to spare from your survival needs, start looking for opportunities to learn and grow. Research your community from top to bottom; find out what is offered, from public lectures to formal training courses. Start with something short, simple, and cheap, perhaps some educational event at church or free in the community. *Go do it* – it will expand your appetite for more!!

Learning can be a reward in itself – but the more focused on your goals the better. So as you get adjusted and have more free time, look around for a source of training that can lead to a new job, a better income, a way to carry out your long-range plans. All it takes to enroll in a community college is a GED and a few bucks, and there you will find lots of good ideas and new people, as well as useful job skills.

A practical reminder: with any new type of job you consider, find out up front if your criminal history will be an obstacle. For example, people with a drug history should not go to truck driving school because they cannot obtain licensing or certification. This kind of barrier exists in many occupations, so be sure to check out your prospects before you invest your resources!

THE ART OF HAVING FUN

"There is MUCH more to life than just surviving! Reach out for creative ways to express yourself and connect with the wonder and power of the Universe."

It doesn't take long in prison to lose your sense of humor, or to forget how to relax and have fun. As you know, fun dies behind bars, and you can become an awfully sad and dull person. Upon release it is natural to bring a lot of this flat, dark view of life and attitude out with you. So what do you do?

It may sound strange but "having fun" after imprisonment is another special skill that has to be developed. If necessary, you need to force yourself to go out and acquire fresh, positive energy by finding positive people and activities which are safe and enjoyable. At first it will be awkward but stick with it! As with all efforts after prison, it requires faith, time, and effort to replace the poison and pain with a positive passion for life. If you don't do this – if you stay inside your shell and hide – nothing will change ... you will remain distant from life *exactly like an inmate in an isolation cell.*

Refuse to be chained to the past! Now that you are in the free world it is *essential* that you seek out creative ways to enjoy your new life. A lot of events and chances for personal enjoyment are listed in the weekend section of most daily newspapers or on the Internet. We assume that fun requires money, but this isn't always true. After years in a prison recreation yard, just a walk in a real park or sitting by a lake can be an absolute joy! Being free to do things,

no matter how trivial, can be a tremendous pleasure.

It helps to think of the community as a *treasure chest of opportunity.* Reach out for new experiences and relationships that are rewarding for you and positive for the world around you. Along with enjoyment, this brings you *new, clean power,* a way to recharge your personal battery after release. A good way to do this is to develop friendships in which you share good times or common interests. It is worth the time and effort required because being with good people is one of the supreme rewards of living!

Your new freedom also brings the chance to be private, a long awaited relief from years of prying eyes. Now you can rediscover the meaning of peace and quiet, so essential to a person's well-being. Make time to be by yourself, listen to your inner voice and the natural sounds around you.

Having fun has some practical benefits: it reduces your stress levels and offers proof that there is more to life than grief and misery. Real enjoyment doesn't come easily, but don't make a job of it. Just look for positive ways to "lighten up." *Be glad to be alive and let yourself enjoy all aspects of your freedom!*

GIVING BACK

"Nothing is more satisfying than helping others. When done with purity of heart, it lifts us up and makes our lives worthwhile!"

There is no better method of moving forward than by reaching back to help someone else advance in life. No matter how modest the effort, you will find that rendering service to others results in priceless benefits of dignity and self-worth. Plus, we have a duty to "give back" to the world the kindness and support that others have given us along the way.

However, let's be practical ... during the first two years after release, you will need to devote most of your efforts to pulling your own life together. After all, you can't give what you don't have. But the day will come when you do have some extra time and energy, and there is no better way to use it than by helping someone less fortunate or advanced than you. Volunteer a little time to help those around you; the rewards are *significant.*

This could be something as simple as helping a neighbor who is ill or offering your services through a church or agency. One thing to remember: many volunteer agencies now run background checks on people to see if they have a criminal history. So you need to be totally upfront when you apply and not take it personally if an organization turns you down. Above all, you should not seek to work in any situation which is related to the type of charges that lead to your arrests or convictions. Also, if you are on parole, it's smart to clear your volunteer activity in advance with your P.O. These steps will help assure that your noble intentions do in fact have noble results.

As you apply yourself to assisting others, the changes you have experienced in the criminal justice system take on a positive purpose. This gives your life far greater meaning, and finally the day comes when you snap to the fact that prison was something you *had* to go through to get where you are today!

Positive Outcomes

■ *A Person of Worth – YOU*

"The person you will become depends on the quality of your values and actions now. What matters most is that you seek to be decent, kind, and fair."

Many wonderful things result from hard work, faith, and patience. One important measure of success comes when we gain the respect of others. But if we want the world to respect us, we first must respect ourselves. This is easier said than done, especially for those of us who have caused physical pain and emotional distress. In fact, I believe that all who read this book will, if we are honest, find things that make us feel sad and even shameful about ourselves and our actions.

But the good news is you now have the opportunity to improve and expand yourself by changing the way you think and act. One of the real rewards of life after prison is that each new day of freedom gives you another chance to increase your self-respect and take on a new identity as "a person of worth." This can't be wishful thinking or a cheap boast. Each person who re-enters the free world must *truly believe* that he or she can make it and be *absolutely committed* to paying the price to achieve success.

Can it happen overnight or just because you want it to? No, of course not, but it *can be done and you can do* it!! After being a puppet for so long, it's time you start pulling your own strings. Time to take control of the greatest challenge in the universe: *your true self*. What better place than a cell to learn the harder facts of life ... to truly "understand" that you can and must take control of your own fate?!

Prison strips away a *lot* of the garbage you've collected in the past. You walk out naked – newborn after a long and difficult delivery – so vulnerable and yet so filled with potential. Use your experience in the criminal justice process to look deep within and to grow against all odds. In the free world, the choices you make will determine who you are and what direction you will take. And each day you will have just a little more control over your future.

By accepting responsibility for your values and actions, you become the master of your fate. It doesn't always matter if others recognize the positive nature of your efforts – it's what *you* know about your good intentions and sense of honor that is important. And, unlike physical objects, no one can take from you the satisfaction of knowing you are doing the best you can. Remember, your final goal is to grow, prosper, and replace the pain with peace. And in case no one ever tells you again, *you can do it!!*

■ *Ours to Make or Break*

"The world owes us nothing ... ABSOLUTELY NOTHING! Our lives are OURS to make or to break, so the future is based on our choices, large and small."

As any inmate knows, life in the joint takes existing problems and makes them ten times worse! But, despite all the madness you have gone through, I assume you are determined to take control of your life.

If you're like me and thousands of other ex-cons, much of the heart break you've endured has come from your own misguided thoughts and deeds. Even if someone set you up and violated your trust, it couldn't have come down without your active participation! By now you are ready to face this fact and take charge of what you think and do. At some point during your captivity, you reached that moment of enlightenment when "enough is enough." From then on you silently dedicated yourself to do what is required to live a positive, rewarding future! This means taking ownership of your actions and their effects on you and others ... *this is freedom!!*

As an ex-con fresh out of a cell, you know you can't afford to wait for the government or anyone else to help you in your quest to change from "loser" to "winner." After all, you are the one who has to live with yourself and the results of your actions. If you want it done, *you do it!!* Accepting this reality sets you free as nothing else can.

So your life is YOURS! You were not born a slave, nor destined to live under the control of someone or something else. No matter what you have done or what has been done to you, refuse to let your life be consumed by what is already dead and gone! This decision liberates you from your negative history, letting you focus instead on making use of the positive lessons you have learned.

The present is the only moment in which you can actually change anything. So as you gradually shift your focus from past mistakes to present accomplishments, you will feel a great burden lifting from your shoulders. By operating in the "here and now," you have the right, the responsibility, and finally the chance to improve your daily life. *Use it well!!*

◼ *Another Day FREE*

"What 'freedom' means to an ex-con is the opportunity to be alive!! Alive to experience small wonders that others take for granted; alive to make a contribution to the world; alive to know joy and be at peace."

By now you know not to expect any miracles during the first 24 months following release. In this early stage of reconstruction, mere survival is a major victory and your ongoing progress a reward in itself. As time passes your life will expand to include much more; but for now just be happy that you wake up each morning in the free world.

Acknowledge that each day is a triumph and pace yourself like a long-distance runner. The first nine months are best lived "one day at a time." If you do this well, the next

nine months you can stretch out to one week segments. By the time you hit 24 months, your control and endurance will have so improved that you will be living one month at a time. At last, most of the extreme madness and panic will be over.

A word of caution: as you approach the third year, some really heavy things begin to happen which can do you great damage. Now that your survival is taken care of, it is all too easy to get lost because you don't know how to shift gears. You notice yourself becoming increasingly bored and frustrated ... just getting by isn't enough! You want MORE ... but you don't really know how to break free of the past and move forward into a new day. Most ex-cons go through a major crisis about now. You are likely to get loose and do something very stupid – so stupid it either destroys you or scares you so badly you tighten up your act and dedicate yourself to another year of progress and growth.

By 48 months you will realize that although you still have a long way to go, you are well on your way to true, lasting freedom. During this period, your job is to achieve long-awaited stability and the first hint of balance. For the first time since release, you start to feel that you actually have some real control over today and tomorrow.

Then, the very day you complete your sixtieth month, take time to celebrate and congratulate yourself on a job well done!! This doesn't mean your struggles will be over. But you have lived through the worst and passed a major milestone. Although you still have to deal with your past, your future efforts will have more to do with life in the community and less and less to do with the criminal justice system.

Many times across this five-year period you will feel worn out and fed up with it all. When this happens, stop and remind yourself that everything you do is an investment in the years to follow. Through all the ups and downs, keep a clear sense of your purpose – to achieve and constantly increase your control over your fate. You see, when you meet your goal of five years arrest-free, you have gained two rewards: first, you are free of your past and, most important, you are free to pursue an ever higher quality of life. So take your dreams of dignity, comfort, peace, and joy and make them real!!

■ *True Liberation*

"Just as you counted the months to release, every new month of freedom moves you farther away from prison and ever closer to the true liberation of your mind and heart. Stick with it … never, ever give up!!"

By the time you reach 60 full moons of freedom, you will be a totally different person from the one who is currently reading this book.

Most of the insane flashbacks will be over – along with the stress and confusion of life after prison. Much of the uncertainty and insecurity of day-to-day living will also be resolved, and in its place will be a strong, vibrant, well-earned sense of *purpose, pride, and achievement.*

With this greater stability, you can focus on improving the quality of your daily life, moving upward and onward, meeting and conquering new, exciting challenges. True liberation means you now have the will and ability to make constructive use of the past, while facing the present with expanding confidence and satisfaction.

Above all, maintain faith in your ability "to make things right and good," no matter what adversity you face! Your vision of a better world will slowly transport you from a past of grief and pain to a higher, more rewarding level of existence. This has worked for me and many others … just as it will for you!!

THIRD
for the family and loved ones who waited ...

▨ *Concern for the Future*

It's been a long hard grind, but your loved one is *finally* coming home within the next six months or so. Bet you wondered if it would ever happen. It certainly has been a long time and there have been a lot of changes in both of your lives during the time you've been separated. But you're very relieved that it's almost over and your loved one is returning soon. What's that? *You're happy, but ...?* Just what do you mean, *but?* Is there a note of hesitation there?

You say you're pleased, but you're just not sure ... not sure about anything any more? Are you worried what he or she will do when released? Afraid you'll be put through hell *all over again?* Worried about the quality and future of your relationship?? You say you're confused and a bit frightened – you even feel *guilty* because you shouldn't feel this way at all???

Well, put your mind at rest. Yours is a perfectly normal reaction to an abnormal situation. *You're not alone* in experiencing these doubts and uncertainties. In fact, your loved one is probably going through similar feelings and frustrations right now.

It's important for you to understand that what you are experiencing is the next step through the maze ... and *you're close to the door!* Now is the time for you and your loved one to discuss the forces which are pushing and pulling on *both* of you in different ways. Then look for ways to gain understanding of your feelings and how best to cope with them.

▨ *Short Time Blues*

You and your loved one are going through a period of adjustment at this time known as "gate fever" or "short pains." This simply means that an inmate has a brief time remaining to serve in confinement and will soon be coming home – usually within 180 days or less. *Many* mental and physical changes occur during this period and, like it or not, you too are experiencing some of the same symptoms. You are suffering as much as, if not more than, your loved one.

If you have read the first part of this book, you know your loved one is going through a lot of adjustments right now. You may have picked up on this during your recent visits or perhaps by reading between the lines of letters. In any event, you do know that *something strange is stirring!* But what about yourself? Just

71

how are *you* holding up? Remember, while your loved one in prison is feeling pressures, you are also experiencing many of these same pressures, as well as some problems unique to you. Why?

First, a series of major changes is about to occur in your life and you are worried that you may not be able to control the situation the way you want. Second, you're worried about the welfare and fate of someone you care about and wish the best for. Third, you have many emotional scars after years of involvement in the madness and pain of your loved one's criminal behavior and imprisonment; you are secretly worried that he or she has not "seen the light" as you have repeatedly been promised. Last, you are tired, bone tired, of this whole situation and are praying for relief.

All this combines like a storm cloud within your heart which you try to fight off with hope and optimism. This conflict between hope and fear is creating the stress you are experiencing.

▎*Shifting Gears*

Think back to the time your loved one first went to prison. Remember the adjustments you *both* had to make in your lives at that time – the hassles, the stress and uncertainties? Who could forget, right? Well, you now have got to do it all over again, but *this time in reverse.*

Seems as though you were finally getting some order back in your life without your loved one being present, and now you've got to turn around and rearrange everything again. All of those old doubts and

fears emerge and take hold on your life. But now, you've got some new ones to consider: how much has your loved one changed; how much have *you* changed; what about the kids, the neighbors, relatives? How are you going to cope with this expanding stress? When will it stop? So much anxiety mixed with excitement and fear of the unknown ... what *a mess!*

Keep in mind that your loved one is going through many of these same changes. The shorter the time to release, the more tense you *both* become. The first danger in this is an increasing breakdown in communications between the prisoner, you, and the world. And it couldn't come at a more inappropriate time. Right now, you both need to draw upon all the inner resources you can muster to make a successful transition from confinement to freedom. Keep in mind that this release is social and personal rebirth ... the beginning of a new life ... a fresh start! *Courage and determination are essential!*

▎*Stability Is Crucial*

At this point, you should be cautious when you discuss any long-term plans with your loved one. Instead, you *should* discuss short-term behavior, individual expectations, and simple plans for finding quiet ways to get to know each other again. In this transition period, the excitement and fears of the upcoming release keep you from carving the future in stone. But you *can* make "verbal contracts" so that you have a better understanding of your common goals, attitudes, and actions.

It is very common for the loved one of an inmate to fall into an *intense emotional depression* due to the fear of what will happen once the prisoner is free again to roam the streets. Please remember that the cause of this is *uncertainty ... pure anxiety* from not being able to control the future or predict your loved one's success or failure following release.

You may feel your mind is running a million miles a minute as you try to predict and prevent every possible disaster that might affect your loved one before and after release. This will leave you mentally and emotionally exhausted, drained of all energy. These conditions make it hard for you to think clearly and come to good decisions. If at all possible, you should postpone important decisions that involve major emotional, social, or financial investments until your life and your emotions settle down.

Even if you are normally a stable, level-headed person, you may experience severe stress during this time. Stress may show in different ways, some familiar to you, some unexpected. You may be angry, irritable, intolerant of family or co-workers, forgetful, anxious, afraid, so nervous you feel like jumping out of your skin. Some people experience stress as headaches, back trouble, stomach upsets, tightness of breath, nausea, or diarrhea. You may feel just fine and think you are handling the situation with no problems. If so, be very aware of your inner feelings. You may be holding your stress inside. This can cause health problems such as ulcers or heart trouble.

There is no foolproof way to defuse such stress. It is created by the situation you are in and will go away as you pass through it. Meanwhile, you must recognize that the stress is there and find ways to cope. You may try exercise, quiet walks, music, relaxation tapes, meditation, a soak in the tub. Spend time with people who make you laugh. Avoid people who criticize or give uninformed advice. It's a good idea to tell your friends about the strain you're undergoing. This will help them to be more understanding of your moods.

If you feel like you're going crazy, you know just how your loved one in prison feels. You can help each other by sharing your insights and methods of coping. When your loved one is irritable or unreasonable, be aware that it is the short pains talking. And ask him or her to be understanding when *you* are tense. It is very important for your loved one *and* your relationship that you be honest and keep your channels of communication open right now.

Do all you can to keep yourself physically, mentally, and spiritually balanced at this sensitive time. And do not hesitate to reach out for help! Seeing a counselor, taking a class on stress management, or going to a doctor may help you get through this period with the health and strength to face your new challenges. If you know others who are facing the same experience, their understanding and support may help you gain some peace and a new perspective on your problems. *Take good care of yourself!!*

▇ *So Many Lives*

Although these feelings are most intense for the spouse or partner of a prisoner, other family members also have stress, concern, fear, and uncertainty when facing the return of an imprisoned loved one. There may be many resentments built up over past hurts and injuries. Parents may have paid tremendous sums for legal fees, bonds, fines, restitution, wrecked cars, treatment centers – money they will probably never recover. Siblings have experienced embarrassment and pain for the harm the inmate's actions have caused. Siblings may also resent the time and money parents have expended on the prodigal child who has injured the family and now, they think, expects a homecoming celebration.

In some cases, disagreement over how to deal with the inmate has already led to family problems and even break-ups. Parents may have divorced; resentment may develop between parent and step-parent or between siblings and parents; family members may stop seeing and speaking to each other, as some support and continue the relationship while others want to bury it.

These issues will not disappear although they may be hidden for awhile during the joyous reunion. As things settle down, these festering concerns need to be acknowledged and discussed, both with the released prisoner and between family members who may have conflicting feelings and material concerns about the return. Discussion may not resolve all the problems or heal all wounds, but it will make the relationships more honest and reduce some of the resentment, at least that of suffering in silence.

▇ *Children's Needs*

Children of returning prisoners have special problems of their own. They may have endured shame, an unstable home life, a sense of abandonment and betrayal, and a negative self-image. They may even have gotten into trouble themselves. They may have conflicting feelings: mixed loyalty to both the caretaker and returning parent, a lack of respect for the absent parent and his or her authority over them, no sense of closeness to the parent who has been absent – often even before imprisonment – as well as more practical concerns, such as where they will live.

Children need to be reassured that they are loved and will have stability and protection. They may be fearful, resentful, or rebellious at first; they need time to adjust and get to know the returning parent. In some cases, a gradual introduction may be the wisest approach. If these transitions are difficult or don't seem to be working out, it may be wise to seek help from a family counselor.

New Friendships

▇ *How the Relationship Will Change*

There are going to be many changes in your lives – both for you and for your loved one – and they're going to happen very soon. But when you both have a bad case of the short pains, everything is too focused on the immediate moment of *release*. Don't forget that the experience coming *out* of prison is just as demanding as *going in*. It is a period of rapid, unexpected change which seems to lack both purpose and stability. Your lives may seem to get harder for a while, just when you thought they would get easier. *But this will pass* as you have a chance to re-define and adjust to one another and to freedom over the first year following release. Be patient.

The relationship you had with your loved one before he or she went to prison changed as you both adjusted to the many burdens of prison life. Now your relationship will take many new turns. The best way to cope with the confusion is to agree to work together to build a *new friendship* – to re-define and re-direct the ways you deal with one another. This means that you must agree to construct a brand-new relationship built on a foundation of respect and honest concern.

▓ *Building a Healthy Bond*

It is helpful to review what goes into building a strong, positive connection between people. Many experts agree that the following characteristics are signs that a relationship works well for the people in it.

- *Open, honest communication* – Members are comfortable talking to each other honestly about how they feel on many topics. They talk *to* each other, not *about* each other. There are no issues that are off limits or too scary to discuss.

- *Ability to share deep inner feelings* – Members are free to talk about their most personal feelings, no matter what they are: anger, fear, joy, caring. Their feelings are acknowledged and accepted as being real, even if other members do not agree.

- *Effective patterns of problem solving* – Members are willing to admit when they have problems, and work together to solve them.

- *Fair allocation of power and decision making* – Members share power and make decisions together, rather than competing to control the relationship. If there is disagreement, they negotiate until they find an acceptable compromise.

- *Real liking and respect* – Members care about one another's well-being. They encourage, rather than criticize, even if one makes a mistake. Members feel safe to be themselves.

- *Closeness and individualism* – Members respect and encourage each other's uniqueness, without letting their differences threaten their sense of togetherness. No one assumes that they know how the other feels; each person is responsible for knowing and expressing his or her own needs and feelings.

- *Sharing and accepting responsibility* – Members work together to achieve common goals and help each other achieve their individual goals. Each person realizes they are responsible for their own choices and actions; they don't blame their mistakes or problems on each other.

- *Shared values* – Members have a core of beliefs, values, commitments, and goals that they hold in common, even while they respect individual differences.
- *Flexibility and tolerance of change* – Members have common goals, routines, etc., but they are not rigid. They can agree to change plans and head in a different direction without too much stress or discomfort.
- *Openness to the outside world* – Members feel comfortable interacting outside the relationship and inviting others into their home and activities.

Of course, working to build a fresh, healthy relationship will in itself create a lot of stress. This is one reason it is so important that you proceed with caution. It will take time and hard work; everyone involved must have a strong commitment to make the relationship better. The main building blocks will be honesty, willingness to communicate, and a positive, caring attitude.

As you are working to build a new relationship, you may be surprised to find yourself resenting the very changes you want to make. While your loved one has been away, you have worked hard to build a new life for yourself. You may have taken on a lot of new responsibilities and are proud of your strength and independence. Naturally, you don't want to give up the things you have worked so hard to achieve. Now that your loved one is coming home, you may

fear that he or she will not respect or approve of the new you. You may even resent his or her demands on the time, money, and possessions you have earned. He or she may seem like an intruder in your home and your life.

This is a time of *confusion* – such conflicting thoughts and feelings are to be expected. Shared values and goals will help see you through this fog and establish a clearer look into the future. It helps to discuss with your loved one his or her goals and to express your own concerns, both short- and long-range. You may find your loved one pleased that you have grown and changed. He or she may be relieved to share responsibilities in a new way. At the same time, if you want to build a future together, you must be prepared to share your life in a way that feels fair to you both.

You may feel very reluctant to let your loved one back into your life and home if he or she has abused your trust in the past. You need to be completely honest and up front about this long before the release date. You have the *right* to decide that you don't want your loved one to live with you. If you make this decision, you can help him or her develop another plan for where to live after release. This may sound hard, but *many* released prisoners have no family to return to. They find a way to live, and so must your loved one. No matter how you feel, you are responsible for *yourself only*, just as your loved one is responsible for his or her own life.

If you decide that your loved one will live with you, you may feel safer if you have an agreement, verbal or in writing, as to each person's expectations and responsibilities. You should have a clear understanding as to what will happen if the agreement is broken. And be ready to follow through. If you don't make it stick, you are just encouraging the abuse to start all over again.

But do *not* start by laying down rules and regulations on how you expect your loved one to behave once home. Many family members are so up tight about the future actions of their loved one, they overreact and try to enforce strict controls for their own peace of mind. This is understandable but *it won't work!* You must be prepared to greet your loved one as a responsible adult. If he or she hasn't grown up in prison, *you* won't be able to change him by your rules. Once you have negotiated an agreement that seems fair, your best tool is *encouragement.* Let your loved one know that you are prepared to offer suggestions and help only when he or she *wants* your help.

If a former prisoner grows to see you as an extension of the jail or penitentiary, he or she will simply ignore you or react with rebellion and hostility. You will lose the ability to communicate and rebuild your relationship.

▓ *Don't Be a Sucker*

This doesn't mean you should sit silently by while a former prisoner engages in destructive or criminal behavior. Encourage your loved one to *be and act in a responsible manner.* Don't nag, just be very honest and direct in a concerned and respectful way. Remember: under no circum-

stances should you permit yourself to become a physical or emotional victim. If this should occur, seek professional guidance and support immediately. *Your* health and well-being, on all levels, must be a top priority. There is ***never*** any justification for abusive behavior *on any level* of your relationship.

Devote your time and energy to remaining calm and preparing yourself, mentally and physically, for the events of the next few months. There will be up times and down times, good times and bad times; you'll need all your strength to cope.

Overcoming False Expectation

▓ *The Universal Demon*

As we discussed in earlier sections, two major problems which crop up between the offender and loved one are illusion and false expectations. These are often the basis of *serious* misunderstandings and problems with personal relationships during and following incarceration. They can only be overcome by thinking realistically, planning realistically, and acting realistically. In other words, you must know the difference between dreams and illusions.

The first big false expectation, for both inmates and their families, is that all their problems will be over when the offender walks out the gate. This is definitely not true. You know this in your mind but emotionally you just want it to be over! In reality, the hard work of adjusting to the free world and building a rewarding relationship is just beginning. There may be times when your life gets harder before it gets better. There will be another mouth to feed the very first day, but it may take some time before your loved one can find a job to help meet these new expenses. Or he or she may be sent to a halfway house, when you were expecting him home.

The second false expectation is that you fully know the person coming home. The prison experience forces inmates to adapt to a lifestyle we do not often confront in the free world. You get glimpses of these changes in your letters and visits, but you can't see a whole person in such small pieces. This doesn't mean that all of the changes will be for the worse. And it doesn't mean that your loved one intends to hide anything from you; he or she may not be aware of the changes or may not be able to put them in words. It *does* mean that you can't take this person for granted. Be prepared for some surprises. And remember that *you* have changed, too. Your loved one will have to get acquainted with the new you.

■ *"Jail House Loves"*

In the case of "jail house love affairs," where a man and woman build a special bond despite – in the face of – the entire prison experience, some truly unique and conflicting realities apply. Jail house love is intense! It's painful, dramatic, and *far heavier* than any soap opera will ever be. Because of its intensity, it often has almost magical influences on those involved. It's hard to know how such very powerful bonds are born under the shadow of a gun turret in a visiting yard and between the lines of an endless stream of letters. For some, it becomes a full-time crusade, a painful, passionate, intoxicating quest ... with *release* seeming to hold the golden key to eternal happiness.

In some ways, you have shared so much of yourselves that you feel almost like one person. But other parts of you may be totally foreign to each other. This is understandable; people caught up in very hard situations try to maintain a relationship by offering each other only the very best of themselves. Often daily attitudes and ways of doing things are set aside until after release ... *then comes the moment of truth.*

It is not realistic to expect instant union and bliss. You must allow time for your unknown parts to become acquainted. Remember: *nothing* involved in the "correctional experience" is normal, natural, or sane. It is essentially impossible to get an honest look at the future while still looking at the world through bars.

No matter what the nature or history of a person's relationship with another, certain building blocks are absolutely essential. For a jail house love to survive, it has to be redefined based on the rules of the game as it is played *on the streets, here and now.*

The Influence of Love

■ *Your Power to Help*

There's no doubt that you have learned much during the time your loved one has been in prison. You now will have the opportunity to put it to good use. You will need to maintain a positive attitude through the demanding times that lie ahead. *The negative has no place in your life.* Your loved one is going to need all the love and understanding you can give as he or she makes the transition from the agony of confinement to the responsibilities of freedom. You can't force him to do it; you can't do it for her. You simply can offer encouragement and support as he or she works through the many adjustments.

Your attitude toward your loved one's future after release can have a *major influence* on his or her own sense of worth. Do your best, in an honest way, to radiate confidence! I don't suggest you be a sucker for anyone, or that you should be too weak to face the cold reality of a person's deceptive practices – only that you be *objective* and *supportive* when your loved one is of good intent and making a good-faith effort to be legal and ethical.

■ *Truth with Compassion*

How many times after reading a letter from your loved one in prison have you wanted to say, "Get real!" Or in the visiting room, when he or she would talk about the future, a future you knew was far more wishful thinking than realism? This puts you in a bad spot: what do you do? Do you confront him or her with "how things really are" or be silent because you don't want to seem negative and you figure a prisoner needs to hold onto any hope they can find?

Perhaps the best approach is to

say, *"That's a great idea. Have you thought about how you are going to prepare to achieve that goal now and after release?"* Then you are in a position to help discover and define the skills, time, etc. needed to turn this dream into reality. If a person's ambition really is an illusion, he or she will come to that conclusion on their own.

After release is different; no one has a lot of time or patience for anything except what is real and practical. This is when you must be "real" but supportive ... offer truth with compassion. This is best done by open, honest discussion between friends, looking at the pros and cons of a given situation. You should not give instructions or try to make decisions for your loved one. All you can do with anyone is share good information and wish them the best.

The Moment of Release

■ *Home Again, Home Again*

Hooray! Now what? Sure, it was *wonderful*, those first few days when he or she came home. But now what? *So much change!* Nothing seems the same as before. Your loved one has changed and *you* have changed – more than you had expected – and it's been quite a shock to you!

Just remember, for the first few weeks, *everyone* remains in a mild state of shock and depression. This is generally followed by some disorientation and mistrust. A renewed sense of life and belonging comes as a slow result of consistent hard work. But these stages are *predictable parts* of the "correctional experience." To get a better understanding of what is going on, read the section *"Survival on the Roller Coaster"* earlier in the book.

If you and your loved one stay stuck in the stage of post-release confusion, you may be left with a sense of alienation that is both long-lasting and destructive. Willingness to share your deepest feelings with each other will help you pass through this isolation into a sense of being connected with each other and the rest of the world.

At times ex-inmates seem to make a fairly easy transition to freedom, but in reality this is simply not true. Many problems exist, if you know what to look for. It is likely they are holding themselves in tight check, not able to comprehend that they really are free, or just not knowing what to do about it! A calm surface may also be a sign of profound shock. If this is the case, the real adjustments may start several months after release. In the meantime, the family can help by being patient and supportive and not putting heavy expectations and pressures on their loved one.

■ *Intimate Concerns*

If you are the spouse or mate of a newly released prisoner, you will probably find it's difficult having sex with a "stranger" or that sexual experiences are awkward or uncomfortable. If so, *it's perfectly OK* because you need to get to know the friend and companion you lost when the prison door slammed shut. For those who built their relationship *during* imprisonment, the fear and discomfort with sexual issues

following release can be *extremely* stressful.

No matter what the reason, be honest with your feelings and don't hide behind any excuses or how you think things "should be" based on the illusions created in passionate prison letters. Express your concerns *directly* to your loved one in a way that is sensitive to his or her pride and fears. Many ex-prisoners have great expectations of themselves as lovers, and also great fears that they will not perform as expected. In reality, it is normal for your physical relationship to feel awkward at first. Also remember that stress – the changes you are both going through – has a dampening effect on sexual feelings. Just be tender, keep a good sense of humor, and let nature take its course.

Remember, before all else, the elements needed to build a valuable, rich friendship are *mutual honesty* and *sincere tenderness*. When these elements are present, time and patience will help you to communicate with your bodies what you share within your minds and hearts. You may find it helpful to work together on exercises to increase your sensitivity and ability to communicate about sexual feelings. These are available in self-help books at bookstores or libraries. If you find after a reasonable time that you still have a problem with lovemaking, don't hesitate to talk to a qualified therapist.

■ *Bridge Building Can Be Fun*

Just as it required many months for you to adjust to your loved one's being away, so too will time be required for adjustment coming back home. This adjustment period will weigh heavily on both you *and* your loved one, and generally lasts for a minimum of 18 to 24 months. For prisoners who have served very long sentences, it can take far longer. *There are no short cuts!*

This is a very critical time for you both. You will need to draw upon your strength of character and creative powers to get you through it. Too often the family or loved one of a former prisoner will be so anxious to get the pain of the past behind them that they will expect the newly released person to adjust to the responsibilities of the streets very quickly. Such expectations can be quicksand; *they are not real.*

Work toward daily progress and take pride in small advances and minor achievements. Reconstruction from an experience as powerful and destructive as long-term imprisonment requires *time, work, and dedication* from everyone involved. Just keep your head up. Be strong.

It's natural for your loved one to want some time to sort things out, and rightfully so. However, let your first priority in the three months after release be coping with those *survival* issues needed to pull life together. Focus first on immediate needs such as food, shelter, work. Offer consistent encouragement and practical support (transportation, clothes, contacts) in the search for employment. A suitable job must be one of your loved one's first goals, and, for a person with a felony conviction, jobs are very hard to come by. It would help if you and your loved one each get OPEN's book *Man, I Need a Job!* (see the back of this book for information) so you can refer to it before and after release. When you have the same base of information, you can better understand and discuss the special problems associated with getting and keeping a job with a criminal history.

After these immediate needs are met, you can begin to look down the road at what you both view as a fresh, meaningful life. When you have developed common goals and worked together to achieve them, you have begun the process of creating a happier, more satisfying relationship. Recognize that every successful step, no matter how small, is a big achievement because it helps to build faith in the future and thereby creates a strong foundation for a richer, more fulfilling life.

Work *together* finding new ways to have fun. Be creative and enjoy each other while getting things settled and back on track. However long your loved one was locked up in prison, he or she had no privacy, no peace and quiet. Respect his or her need to enjoy some regular periods of private time and space, and recognize that you need these things, too. You will find that time to be your individual selves will enrich your relationship as you learn to share a new life together.

You may become tired of listening to "war stories" about your loved one's experiences in prison or want to scream next time you hear things that begin with, "In the joint we ...." This happens because a newly released prisoner cannot yet identify with the community and simply has nothing else to talk about for awhile. Be patient; this will slowly diminish as your loved one grows more connected with daily life in the free world.

And don't waste your energy trying to play "catch up" for all the good times you missed sharing together. It just cannot be done and will lead to many unnecessary frustrations. It is far better to spend the time getting to know one another and sharing mutual respect for each other. Don't dwell on the past. Look toward the future – toward a new life, a fresh start!

▇ *You Can Do It!*

Seek a higher quality of life by sharing new and constructive thoughts and experiences – small things which provide each new day with a growing degree of comfort and satisfaction. The best way to get over the criminal justice experience is to outgrow it!!

As the loved one of a former prisoner, you have paid a high price for your concern. Now devote your energy to building a fresh, wholesome relationship and *look forward to a better way of life*. *You've earned it!*